A View from Iraq

By

Elmer L. Snow, III

PublishAmerica
Baltimore

First printing

ISBN: 1-4241-5784-6
PUBLISHED BY PUBLISHAMERICA, LLLP
www.publishamerica.com
Baltimore

Printed in the United States of America

A NAME FOR ALL MY TEARS

If only I could tell you, how much you meant to me
Wish that I could hold you, then two as one we'd be
I wish that I could tell you, of how I've coped with fears
To share with you my secret, of naming all my tears

A tear for each and every month, lies upon my chest
Eleven more for the fateful day, when you went to rest
As those tears kept falling down, just like pouring rain
Those tears I gave a name to, I named one for my pain

My days are filled with longing, and selfish thoughts of you
Remembering all the things we did, and things we wanted to
I lie in bed and pray to God in heaven up above
A tear just fell upon my chest, I named it for our love

Love and pain, loss and sorrow landed on my heart
Each a tear, a silent thought of you and I apart
I know that you're in heaven, with those you yearned to see
This tear just fell, I held it and, I called it misery

Someday the names will change I hope, I have to wait and see
Faith and hope, laughter, smile, a tear named charity
But now I know you'll understand, there is no tear for fate
And God won't let me shed a tear and name it after hate

If only I could tell you how much you meant to me
If you were here for one last time, I know I'd make you see
The value of your friendship, your love, my precious dear
Until we meet, I'll think of you, through naming all my tears

Chapter 1

On May 1, 2003, the President of the United States, George W. Bush, declared an end to the Iraq war. Five days later, on May 5, 2003, the author was contacted by Walter Youngblood of Halliburton Corporation in Houston, Texas, and offered employment in Baghdad, Iraq, on a one-year contract.

Youngblood requested that I immediately send a resume that would provide my background and experience for the position.

What was the position? I would be a VIP/Executive Driver for retired Lieutenant General Jay Garner, who had been selected by the President to lead the American Coalition in the rebuilding of Iraq.

Making a decision to travel to Iraq under the best of conditions would be difficult. I realized that General Garner would be a primary target for any Iraqi who held a grudge, and further realized that there were perhaps hundreds of Iraqis who would welcome an opportunity to kill the highest-ranking American civilian in their country. My previous training and experience had always taught me that during an attack, the first target is the bodyguard who's driving or accompanying the V.I.P.

My final decision came during a discussion with my wife when she reminded me that I'd spent my entire life in preparation and training for this type of an assignment. You don't prepare as I'd done, just to decide to sit on the bench when the game has gone into overtime.

We discussed every aspect of relocating, at my age, to a war zone. There was only one decision to make.

One doesn't throw away a lifetime of training, experience, and initiative unless they're ready to surrender to the forces that make people old. I decided that Iraq would be a great place to work for a year or so.

Chapter 2

After submitting my resume to Walter Youngblood on May 6, 2003, I immediately received an e-mail that described the position I was being asked to fill.

> To: Candidate for employment as V.I.P./Executive Driver
> Subject: LOGCAP III- VIP/Executive Driver Candidate Qualification Primer
>
> Thank you for considering employment with KBR Government Operations as a V.I.P./Executive Driver. It is necessary for all applicants considering employment with KBR in this important category to meet minimum qualifications standards. With that in mind please read this memorandum very carefully.

Each candidate for V.I.P./Executive Driver employment must understand vehicle dynamics and the driver/vehicle relationship. This understanding will include "vehicle language," driving form, vehicle/driver weight transfer, ocular driving, threshold braking, off-road recovery techniques, tire skid control, vehicle spin recovery, oversteer/understeer control, tire pressure performance/control effects, tire blowout prevention, advanced emergency threshold braking. Further technical driving capabilities required include: techniques of stress management, night, limited visibility and light problem management. Candidates should understand and be able to accomplish: Street-line driving, Lead/Follow (predictable/random routes) techniques, imminent collision driving techniques, SUV emergency handling, forward/reverse 180 degree turning, bootleg and J-turns, precision immobilization technique(s), swerving for avoidance techniques, barricade confrontation and defensive line driving techniques as minimum V.I.P. driver abilities. In addition, each candidate should be familiar with bomb/explosive detection methods and have wet/dry skid pad as well as counter ambush drill practice. High threat/high speed flight driving techniques are essential.

V.I.P./Executive Driver candidates should consider Personal Protection Specialist training very helpful in the accomplishment of their LOGCAP III driving duties. Individuals without recognized Advanced Driver Certification should not apply for the LOGCAP III contract position.

Halliburton could have saved a lot of memorandum space if they'd just stated that they wanted to recruit graduates of B.S.R. Counter Terrorism Driving Training at Summit Point, West

Virginia. I had gone through that training in 1981, and subsequently had become involved in training several other U.S. contractors who had used my training in various parts of the world.

The e-mails between me and Halliburton suddenly turned into a series of desperate phone calls, each asking what the earliest day I could report for orientation in Houston, Texas, prior to my departure for Baghdad. It was finally determined that KBR, the Halliburton subsidiary, would have airline tickets sent to my home in Florida for a departure for Houston on May 12, 2003.

Chapter 3

Boarding a post-9/11 Continental Airlines flight from Tampa, Florida, to Houston, Texas, can be frustrating during the best of times. When one is traveling on a one-way ticket, such as I was during the morning of May 12, 2005, the departure was more rigid that usual. Despite my showing a retired police badge from the Prince George's County, Maryland Police Department, I was practically undressed prior to being advised I was clear to enter the departure terminal.

The flight to Houston was quite uneventful with the exception of my wondering why airline personnel will conduct such an intense show of security, then the flight attendant will demonstrate how to use a seat belt, and when done, will put the seat belt in an open cabinet where it could be used as a lethal weapon to strike someone during the flight.

At 5:00 PM on Monday, May 12, 2003, I sat with 225 other Americans as we attended our first briefing at the Wyndham

Greenspoint Hotel in Houston. Perhaps the most questionable issue during the original briefing was the continued reference by Halliburton personnel that any of us who spoke to the press would be fired immediately. Several of us began to wonder what Halliburton might be hiding, especially since many details of our assignment weren't even known by those present. As for myself, I wasn't about to disclose my assignment to anyone. There is an old theory that when one talks about security, then security is lost. I already knew that my assignment would be dangerous enough without any type of publicity.

The week of the indoctrination went like clockwork. Physicals, safety meetings, personnel orientation, and the dreaded Nuclear, Biological, and Chemical (N.B.C.) training were all covered, as well as filling endless beneficiary forms in the event we may not survive our contract. Yes, we were prepared for weapons of mass destruction.

Unfortunately, during my week of orientation I learned that Lieutenant General (Retired) Garner was being replaced by Ambassador Bremer as the Senior Civil Administrator in Iraq. And, Bremer had his own security detail.

The dilemma was resolved when Steve Pulley, another counterterrorist driving expert, and I were hurriedly transported to the Halliburton office complex where we were offered positions as security coordinators. This meant a substantial raise was received, prior to our departure out of the United States. It also involved a new set of qualifications that were required for the new assignment.

Stan Mann, the Director of Security for Middle Eastern Operations, interviewed Steve and me for positions as security coordinators. My background in law enforcement was a perfect blend for the new assignment. Stan "the man" Mann wanted security personnel who would function in identifying problems, meeting challenges, and developing solutions on issues with the client, the United States military. One of our primary goals would be to ensure that civilian expatriate personnel would be protected by the military while acting in support, and tandem with our armed forces.

As you will learn later, this assignment was almost a Herculean task.

Perhaps the biggest concern I found, after finally knowing I had a position with KBR, was the fact that there were many new expatriates who had attended their orientation two or three weeks prior, yet remained in Houston waiting for flight arrangements that would get them to Kuwait, then on to Iraq. Those delays alone must have cost the U.S. government hundreds of thousands of taxpayer dollars. Most of these new hires would be utilizing their experience as truck drivers to ensure food and supplies were delivered across the country of Iraq to American and Coalition forces. Many of them would not return to their homes.

There was another plus to the delays involved in debarking for Iraq. Since the processing had been completed for scores of personnel, they weren't required to attend the daily classes since their training had been completed. Nothing much left to do, since they weren't earning money, was to sit in the bars of their respective hotels and drink themselves into oblivion. I even found "oblivion" a couple of times before my departure. The extended delays convinced many of the new hires that they just didn't have the financial resources to sit in a government-provided room in Houston, not receiving a salary, and worrying about their families who wouldn't be receiving money for the foreseeable future. Halliburton lost scores of employees due to their lack of preparedness.

Chapter 4

On May 21, 2003, I and approximately 225 new hires boarded Miami Air Flight 601, a charter flight, and left Houston International Airport. At exactly 10:50 PM the wheels of our plane left the tarmac. This was symbolic because once the wheels left the ground, I began earning my pay. The applause from inside the plane was deafening as we began our journey. Later, the boos would be deafening when we landed for refueling in Athens, Greece, only to learn they wouldn't allow us to leave our plane for a "smoke break" while on the ground. I secretly wished that the Greeks would have a less than successful Olympics. In retrospect, at least that one wish was granted.

While flying from Greece to Iraq, our Miami Air pilot announced that the Iranian government had granted our flight permission to fly along the border of Iraq and Iran. It was comforting to be able to look outside our plane and see that we had jet fighters from the U.S. military as they escorted us through danger zones. We also could look below at several oil refineries in Iraq that continued to burn from the war.

At 3:00 AM on May 23, 2003, we landed at Kuwait International Airport and stepped from the plane into oppressive heat and the smell of burning oil. We were later informed that one of the new arrivals for the Halliburton assignment left the Miami Air plane, went to the waiting personnel, and advised that he was terminating his employment and wanted to be on the first flight out of Kuwait. There is no doubt that this request was acted on immediately.

As for me and Steve Pulley, we were transported in a large bus to Camp Arifjan, a massive military complex that had been provided by the Kuwaiti government to the United States military and which was located approximately halfway between the city of Kuwait and the border with Saudi Arabia.

After our processing was completed we were picked up by Steve Yarborough, another security coordinator who would provide most of our briefings and almost never-ending humor. Humor was one thing we needed after flying for a day and a half, then having to work a 14-hour day on our first day in Kuwait.

As our first day progressed Pulley and I learned that we would not be required to stay in tents that were erected in every conceivable spot on Camp Arifjan. We would be billeted at a resort complex known as the Kalifa, approximately 20 minutes' drive from Arifjan, and located on the Persian Gulf. The perks involved with Halliburton security were starting to become apparent. Especially when we learned that the majority of employees were prohibited from visiting Kuwait. Fortunately, our security personnel were allowed to visit the city to ensure our fellow employees weren't there. In short, we were allowed to go wherever we wanted.

The first few days were spent learning the varied procedures involved in working on a high-security military base. It took some adjusting just to get used to being in the gunsights of high-powered military weapons each time we approached the heavily fortified security gates.

On the whole, my initial period in Kuwait was satisfying. We constantly interacted with Halliburton personnel who were either entering the country for eventual travel into Iraq, or had seen enough evidence of their pending assignment that they elected to terminate employment before going into the war zone.

Chapter 5

By June 2003 I had been re-assigned from working at Camp Arifjan to an area known as "APOD" (Aerial Point of Debarkation). This site was located on the perimeter of the Kuwait International Airport and housed (tented) several thousand members of the United States military, and numerous employees of KBR, the Halliburton subsidiary.

Perhaps the most depressing part of this otherwise great assignment was watching the military "Honor Guards" as they unloaded the remains of U.S. military personnel who had died or been killed inside Iraq. Their remains were brought back to Kuwait for preparation to be returned to their families inside the United States, via Dover, Delaware, Air Force Base. Perhaps the only comfort I can bring to those families, whose loved ones made the "supreme" sacrifice to their country, is the fact that at every step of the way, the remains were handled with the utmost of respect, courtesy, and love by those they served with. I'll explain in detail later.

The months of May and June 2003 began to show a distinct pattern of attacks on the American expatriates who had been hired by KBR to drive supplies for our military from Kuwait into Iraq.

Problems began with children who would run onto the roads and highways in efforts to slow the trucks down. Their purpose was to gain attention with a desire that the drivers would throw food, water, or other supplies out the windows to the waiting beggars. Since there was a prohibition against slowing down or distributing foods, many of the children were struck by the trucks. In retaliation, they began throwing rocks at the drivers. There is no doubt that when the final bill for the costs of the reconstruction of Iraq is tabulated, there will be thousands of reports involving broken windshields.

On several occasions I was assigned to escort personnel across the border into areas of Iraq. It never ceased to amaze me that kids were standing at the side of the road, vigorously waving and greeting us, while at the same time using their free hands to throw nails under the tires of our vehicles.

Travel to Camp Bucca, an enemy prisoner of war camp that was located just miles from the Kuwait border, was one of the most intimidating places that I would frequently travel to. Enemy soldiers and terrorists were incarcerated here, and just driving by the fenced area meant that hundreds of the most violent of Iraqi threats would glare at you as you passed, while grabbing their crotches in order to send a "personal" message. "Yeah, fuck you too," was always an immediate mental reply on the part of our personnel.

As time moved on, the insurgents of Iraq learned that when a convoy is slowed down by the youth, they, the insurgents, could drive up next to a tractor and trailer and attempt to force the truck to stop so the load could be hijacked. Needless to say, our drivers were instructed not to stop under any conditions. This pattern led to the insurgents firing automatic weapons into the trucks. We, in security, knew it was a matter of time before an American civilian would be critically injured.

On a daily basis our convoy drivers would leave the safety and security of Kuwait, drive supplies into Iraq, then return with new tales of violence through attacks.

June 27th can be considered one of the most significant dates of the year for me. On June 27, 2003, I was becoming more and more concerned that with the daily increase in attacks against U.S. Military and Coalition personnel, it was only a matter of time until one of our KBR employees would be targeted by Iraqi militants or terrorists for assassination. The following memorandum was prepared for me and submitted to Joe Brown, my security manager, for his information.

APOD RESPONSE TO KBR EMERGENCY EVACUATIONS

The increase in attacks on U.S. and coalition military personnel in Iraq continues to escalate at an alarming rate. There is every reason to believe that it's only a matter of time before a KBR employee will be targeted. The fatal attack in January, 2003 on a civilian contractor in Kuwait clearly reflects the potential dangers our own personnel face. In a serious situation where life may be threatened or death imminent, it is presumable that a KBR employee would be medically evacuated from Iraq or Kuwait, and brought to the critical care facility of the 47th CSH hospital which is located at APOD. This hospital receives most of the critical wounds from the conflict areas. A medical evacuation of a KBR employee would *possibly* leave our local management with knowledge of the name of one of our victims, how the injury may have occurred, but due to the logistics of transporting the victim, the extent of injury or prognosis of recovery may not be known for an extended period of time. Obviously, a lack of knowledge or information on the status or condition of one of our employee's is not a situation which our management would willingly accept.

The security coordinator's office at APOD has cultivated a working relationship with the medical staff at 47th CSH whereas immediate notification could be made at APOD to inform security and management of the arrival of one or more KBR personnel. In turn, the APOD security coordinator would respond to the medical facility to obtain timely and accurate information or victim identification, condition, prognosis, and would immediately relay this information to the APOD post manager, Mr. Charles Cromwell, who in turn would ensure that information is disseminated through his own chain of notification.

Benefits

Timely and accurate information will be available.

In the event of employee demise, the next of kin would appreciate the fact that a co-employee was present and acting in the best interest of the employee and his/her family.

Security could conceivably take possession of "inventoried" property to ensure items are returned to the family.

Hopefully, a KBR employee who is recovering would benefit from this procedure through increased morale and company support. The security coordinator or APOD manager would be able to ensure that the recovering employee has guests, necessary phones to contact loved ones, etc.

A sound program would ensure that rampant rumors are replaced by factual information.

I finished the memorandum at approximately 8:30 PM on June 27, 2003. An effort was made at that time to e-mail the document to Joe Brown, but I learned that the computer system was down. I called him and advised him of the contents of the memorandum and he assured me that he felt it was important enough to forward to our Director of Security in Houston at the Halliburton Headquarters. I returned to my air-conditioned tent after deciding to wait until the next day to forward the document.

I went to sleep feeling that I'd started a procedure rolling which would have a positive effect on any of our employees who might be injured. The sleep was quickly interrupted at 10:10 p.m on June 27, 2003.

"Corky, get over to the chopper pad; we've got a KBR employee who's been shot in the back and is being air evacuated to your hospital," said Joe Brown as I listened on the cellular phone.

Joe informed me that a truck driver who was employed by our company had been shot while on assignment in the vicinity of NAVISTAR, our truck refueling depot on the Iraq/Kuwait border.

Ten minutes later, at 10:25 PM, I was standing in the rear of the 47th CSH medical facility that is adjacent to the Kuwait International Airport flight line, and waiting for the chopper to land. The KBR manager of health, safety, and environment, Bob Egan, and a KBR medical nurse, Lisa Gray, were already standing by.

Egan informed me that the shooting had apparently occurred approximately 30 miles north of the Kuwait border and the victim had been transported by ambulance to NAVISTAR where after some confusion the evacuation "chopper" had picked up the victim, who was expected to arrive momentarily. We waited nervously while scanning the sky for the arrival of our fellow employee.

At 10:35 PM the helicopter came into view. The pilot circled around Camp Wolf, another name for APOD, and quickly landed, at which time the ambulance personnel retrieved the victim and drove him the 200 yards to the emergency room where emergency room personnel were waiting by the entrance of the tented facility. The entire image was reminiscent of watching an episode of the old television show MASH.

I stood by the ambulance as William "Bill" Dover, a KBR truck driver, was removed, placed on a gurney, and quickly taken into the emergency room. With the exception of his socks, all clothing had been removed and Dover's nude body was covered with an aluminum-foil-type temperature-stabilization cover. Mr. Dover's skin color had turned to a chalky white, he appeared to be unconscious, and in my immediate frame of guesswork, was either deceased, or a potential death victim.

For the next hour we stood outside the tented emergency room and watched through a window in the doorway as a medical team worked feverishly to save a human life. In this case, the human life was a co-worker and I realized that it was very possible that I'd been the one to issue him a Kevlar vest that was designed to save his life. Realistically, I knew that the type of weaponry that our victims were encountering in Iraq was much too powerful to be stopped by the vests which were designed primarily for small-bore arms fire.

At one point during the long and worrisome wait, Lisa Gray, our own nurse who had access to the emergency room, briefed us that Mr. Dover had expired on the table, but had been resuscitated. We waited and drank coffee.

At 1:30 AM on June 28th, the attending surgeon, Captain McDonald, briefed me on the surgery. He advised that the surgery had gone well, and William Dover was expected to make a full recovery within a few months of painful recovery. The doctor advised that Dover had sustained a single gunshot wound that had entered the left rear portion of his back, immediately above the waist. The trajectory of the projectile had traveled upward, while inside the body cavity, missing the victim's intestines, and had lodged in the tissue outside the lung. The doctor advised that Dover had sustained recoverable injury to his diaphragm, pancreas, kidney, and lung.

I was then allowed to go into Unit 4 of the intensive care unit and see Mr. Dover as he benefited from the anesthesia following what had to be the most traumatic day of his life.

I decided to remain with Dover for a couple of additional hours as I wanted to be able to inform his family that he hadn't been in pain, and someone he worked with was with him, in the event he didn't recover.

As I returned to my own tent, after briefing Joe Brown, it dawned on me that exactly 29 years earlier, a young detective, Elmer L. Snow III, had been treated for a gunshot wound to the chest at the Andrews Air Force Base in Maryland. A small world, yet a very benevolent God was still looking over his flock.

Two days later I heard that Bill Dover had been flown to another medical facility where he would continue with his road to recovery.

My last report to KBR personnel provides somewhat of an overview of my assignment.

KBR EMPLOYEE SHOOTING

June 28, 2003 @ 0745 hours. Employee William Dover is resting comfortably at 47th CSH. Mr. Dover had a comfortable night and ventilator should be removed at approximately 1000 hours this date.

Suspect (Shooter) apparently was driving a small, white, Nissan type pick up truck which had a red stripe on side. Pulled up next to victim and opened fire with a burst of rounds from an automatic weapon. Shooter then escaped. *It is significant that the victim was in the last vehicle of the convoy, and was apparently attacked from the left rear.*

More information will be posted here as it is received.

Corky Snow
Security Coordinator

Chapter 6

The life of a security coordinator for Halliburton Corporations subsidiary KBR was for the most part boring in the beginning. Many assignments were dull and mundane, yet as time progressed and the experience level increased, Joe Brown, my security manager, began using me for tasks with increased responsibility.

Perhaps the coverage of the attempted murder by terrorists of William Dover was the most instrumental reason for my selection to my next assignment. The area surrounding the Iraq/Kuwait border was increasing in becoming a real hot spot.

Hundreds of drivers from Third World countries were being hired by Kuwaiti businessmen to come to Kuwait and drive supplies, along with the U.S. Army, into Iraq. These drivers who were assigned to convoys along with KBR drivers were becoming an increasing liability during supply movements. It was also becoming apparent that terrorists were replacing the vandals who were content to throw rocks, and were beginning to engage in placing improvised explosive devices (IEDs) along the roadways. Or, they would place several terrorists with automatic weapons in a small pickup truck, pull up next to a vehicle in the convoy, and if the driver refused to stop, the terrorists would open fire.

The area known as NAVISTAR to the military or "Bubba's Truck Stop" to the American expatriates was the beginning point for all convoys that would transport supplies and munitions for our fighting service personnel. It was located at the Kuwaiti border with Iraq, and death was a constant visitor to the area.

Joe Brown called me by cellular phone to present the problems and relied on me to find a suitable solution. Brown had the ability to contact you with a problem and leave you believing that no one, but you, could resolve that problem.

Because of my law enforcement experience, Brown was aware that a good deal of my experience in civilian law enforcement was based on crime analysis planning that would determine where crime were being committed, times and dates of occurrences, and descriptions of the perpetrators. In our discussions, we decided that if victim drivers were thoroughly interviewed, we could ascertain patterns that would assist the military in providing increased attention to specific trouble areas. My assignment would be to debrief the victims and present accurate "guesswork" on when and where the next attack might occur. We would present our projections of when attacks would occur to the military and they would make every effort to "permanently" eliminate the problems.

One area of concern, and an issue that I'd previously become aware of, was the fact that some of our attacked convoys had received less protection from the military than what we'd expected or needed. There was no hard and fast rule among the American Forces on how they would respond to an attack on a convoy. Some units would immediately engage the terrorists when their convoy was attacked, or when an IED was detonated near a convoy. Others would escort the convoy quickly through the trouble area. A growing concern with the security coordinators was the fact that when the enemy wasn't engaged, we could be assured that the same insurgents would attack on another day. As you may imagine, there was a definite need to coordinate with the U.S. military to ensure the unarmed drivers from KBR, as well as the hundreds of drivers from countries such as India, Pakistan, Turkey, Saudi Arabia were provided with as much protection as possible.

Another issue that needed to be addressed was the philosophy of individual drivers. The American expatriates were operating under the concept that during an attack, they should follow the direction of the military personnel. Drivers from other countries conducted their assignments with the philosophy that should their 18-wheelers be destroyed, they would no longer have employment. In short, the third-country national drivers would more likely stop their trucks during an attack, hoping to avoid damage, rather than follow protocol that was established by their military escorts. Perhaps the language barrier was the biggest obstacle that needed to be overcome.

By my being reassigned to "Bubba's Truck Stop," I had an added advantage of having the ability to speak limited Turkish, a reminder to me of my high schools days of attending school in Ankara, Turkey, while my father was employed there by the U.S. government. There was no doubt this would be an asset while debriefing Turkish drivers who were targeted as much as any other nationality.

Joe Brown decided that I should move my quarters from the APOD at Kuwait Airport to another site, Camp Udairi that was located closer to the border with Iraq, yet had availability of computer links that were important in reporting security issues. This would mean that on a daily basis I would commute, across some of the most remote roads of Kuwait, approximately 30 miles to the Iraqi border.

Steve Pulley was at that time working on the Kuwaiti border so he arranged work and living space for me at Udairi, which I will candidly state was a miserable place to be assigned, despite the good food and presence of air conditioning in a pleasant living container. Desert life should be relegated to the nomads who enjoy it.

Chapter 7

By August 2003 I was regularly working the Iraqi/Kuwait border, supervising the departure of convoys into and out of Iraq. I joined with my friend, Steve Pulley, who had been working the border for quite a period of time, and was a great mentor in teaching me the procedures and protocols to follow. On occasion we had high-speed pursuits of each other in returning to Camp Udairi after a day of interviewing victims of terrorist attacks.

Perhaps the experience of my career in the Prince George's County, Maryland, Police Department was utilized more at the Kuwaiti border than at any time during my employment with KBR. I spent hours each day interviewing victims of convoy attacks, writing reports, and submitting suggestions on how our convoy drivers might be better protected. During this assignment it also became obvious that many soldiers in the U.S. Army were performing superior work, but not receiving credit or recognition for their accomplishments. I vowed to commend our troops whenever I observed conduct and actions that appeared to be above and beyond the call of duty.

On August 6, 2003, I submitted a letter of commendation to Captain Lawrence Moran, Commanding Officer of the U.S. Army's 133rd Military Police Company, who at the time was assigned to NAVISTAR.

It was my pleasure to alert Captain Moran that Sergeant Moody Walters, Sergeant Sandy Russo, PFC Reginald Bright, Sergeant Ceaser Boatwright, Specialist Greg Eklund and Specialist Lynda Brown had performed their assignments in an exemplary manner.

These soldiers, while on the Iraq border, had observed an occupant of an SUV walk to a tractor trailer and place a loaded AK-47 into the cab of the truck that was scheduled to depart for Iraq. The soldiers determined that the occupants of the truck were carrying impeccable credentials that indicated they were working a security assignment for KBR. Despite the assuring tone of the paperwork, our American soldiers remained suspicious and requested my presence at the departure area. Upon my arrival I determined that the two drivers, with impeccable credentials, were in fact Syrian nationals who were expressly forbidden to drive in KBR convoys.

In my letter of commendation to Captain Moran, I advised that because of the professionalism, dedication, and enthusiasm of his personnel, a new method of circumventing security personnel had been identified.

It remains a matter of conjecture as to whom the Syrians planned to use their loaded weapon against. One item is very clear. Had the Syrians avoided security, they would have been in an American convoy with many expatriate targets available.

The month of August 2003 provided more problems than solutions were available for. Although every convoy that departed into Iraq from Kuwait was required to be escorted by the U.S. Army, or other Coalition Forces, once the convoys were in Iraq, the situation usually changed.

Pulley and I were continuously faced with decisions on allowing unsafe tractor trailers that were operated by third-country nationals across the border into Iraq. We realized the urgency of getting supplies to our troops, but also realized that if a truck broke down, it would be left by the U.S. military if it wasn't repaired within minutes. A disabled truck meant that the supplies it carried, no matter what the contents, would end up in the hands of a very aggressive insurgency. Fortunately, the trucks driven by Americans were provided by the United States Government, and were ready for the travel.

KBR drivers, the American ones, were paid on an hourly basis. Drivers from the Third World countries were paid by the trip. And, convoys under military escort were notably slower than individual trucks traveling alone. What did this mean to those of us in security? In an effort to increase their productivity, Third World nationals, even though working under contract to KBR, started leaving the umbrella of security with their convoys and attempted to make the journey without escort. They became sitting ducks, especially to the terrorist and criminal element that waited along the roadways of Iraq.

On August 11, 2003, five Iraqi males in an older-model Chevrolet Sedan pulled up next to two 18-wheelers that were proceeding south toward Kuwait. The two trucks, operated by Third World nationals, had gotten out of their convoy in their haste to return to Kuwait to retrieve another load of supplies.

A witness from another American convoy that was traveling in the opposite direction watched as the Chevrolet pulled abreast of the trucks and fired one shot toward the driver side. When the two trucks failed to stop, all occupants opened fire. The end result was the shooting death of Egyptian driver Refat Mohamed and the wounding of a second Egyptian driver, Gamel Mohamed. The insurgents escaped with both trucks.

There were scores of reports involving attacks on third-country nationals (TCNs) and in dozens of cases we were unable to identify the victim drivers. Primarily, they would be left at the side of the roadway, their trucks taken, and in many cases the identifying passports had also been taken by the insurgents.

Those trucks that were originally in excellent condition when assigned to expatriate drivers were soon showing the wear and tear associated with driving the Iraqi highways. More and more trucks were returning to the border from Iraq and the American drivers were reporting gunshot damage to doors, windows, and occasional major damage from improvised explosive devices that had been planted along the routes of travel. If you know someone who transported supplies in Iraq, you may want to give him/her a pat on the back because they faced death on every mile of Iraqi roadway they traveled.

As the end of August approached, problems with the insurgency seemed to increase. It was becoming very obvious that the insurgents were becoming more adept and skilled at their new "craft," which was attacking the drivers who kept the supplies moving into Iraq. What had started as children vandalizing our American convoys was being transformed into a specialization toward killing. We began to learn of dead animals alongside the roadway whose carcasses contained improvised exploding devices. Once hit, the explosion would occur. Then, we learned that cinder blocks were being tied to bridges and would be placed at eye level for an unsuspecting driver to run into. The briefings with our departing drivers took on a new seriousness as incoming reports kept the security staff apprised of new terrorist techniques. One thing we all were becoming aware of. The insurgency in Iraq was becoming more skilled, organized, and very deadly.

Our own American drivers would share techniques they developed along the roadways in avoiding specific problems. They would share their evasive tactics with us, at the Iraqi border, and in turn, we would brief the next outgoing convoy in the new tactic.

Chapter 8

Too often in writing about war, reporters concentrate on the "shock and awe" ability that our troops are known for, and overlook the "care and compassion" aspect that our American soldiers are capable of giving.

On August 23, 2003, Iamaeel Mohamed Saeed Alwaked, a Syrian truck driver, was returning to Kuwait after delivering supplies into Iraq. He was accompanied by eight other vehicles that had elected to separate from the armed protection of coalition soldiers in the belief they could expedite their return to Kuwait.

When the group was approximately 25 kilometers from the Kuwait border, a small white minivan that was occupied by six Iraqi males approached the group of trucks, from the left rear, and at a high rate of speed. The vehicle pulled adjacent to Mr. Alwaked's driver-side door and the insurgents pointed weapons at him while motioning for him to stop his vehicle. Ismaeel increased his speed as his assailants began firing bursts of machine-gun fire into the cab of his truck. Although seriously wounded and bleeding profusely, he increased his speed and flashed his headlights to the drivers in front of him to alert them to the attack.

The group sped toward the safety of the country of Kuwait.

Staff Sergeant Gloria Green of the U.S. Army's 171 MCT and SSG Carol Brockington of the 628 MCT were at the Kuwaiti border, delivering water to their personnel, when they observed a line of trucks driving at a high rate of speed toward the entry gates into Kuwait. As the trucks entered Kuwait and crossed into safety they pulled to the side of the roadway. The last vehicle in the convoy was observed by the two soldiers as the driver stopped in the middle of the road and a critically injured Ismaeel Alwaked fell to the ground from his truck cab.

The two staff sergeants made a quick assessment of the injuries and elected to transport the victim in the rear of their own truck to an area where a medical evacuation helicopter could safely land to transport Alwaked to a hospital.

While waiting for a medical evacuation helicopter to arrive, these two soldiers spent over an hour in the back of a military truck, and in temperatures nearing 125 degrees, provided first aid while comforting Mr. Alwaked.

Despite obvious fatigue, neither soldier stopped their emergency care until the victim was safely loaded into an evacuation flight.

In my opinion, I didn't see any way that Alwaked could recover from his wounds. I waited for word in Kuwait that he'd expired. Perhaps just as troubling was wondering how he, a Syrian, had managed to transport supplies for KBR.

Following the successful air evacuation of the Syrian driver, I immediately wrote a Letter of Commendation to Captain Christine Habbout, Commanding Officer of the 171st MCT and requested she notify her own superiors about the performance of duty of Green and Brockington.

On August 27, 2003, an Arabic interpreter arrived at the Kuwait border and presented a newspaper article that had been published in

Kuwait, and was written in the Arabic language. There can be no greater tribute to Green and Brockington than to copy that article exactly as it was interpreted.

"Firstly, I want to thank God and U.S. Army that whom save my life without knowing who I am."

"So with these words, Ismaeel-AlWaked starting his conversation with the newspaper after he gets out from intensive care and when they feel that his condition is OK to know what's happened for him". He said, "on the last Saturday when I was come back from Iraq to Kuwait, after I sent all what I can and when I reached Zouber Bridge, I saw that there is a small white van coming behind me and it was coming so fast and when I am trying to check who's the driver for this fastly car, I found three persons and they were hiding their face and they were point for me with their weapons and they asked me to stop, but I didn't do that and I continue driving with high speed than them but they insist to follow me and they shoot me from my back to push me to stop the vehicle." "I tried many times to crash them to leave me alone but they were insist also to kill me but when they found that I will become near Abdali Gate (Kuwait Border) so they run and left me." "And I called a friend of mine and told him what's happened with me and he talk with U.S. Army and they are going to fast to save me once I reached the gate and they took me by helicopter to the hospital to make surgery for me, they are really did that and they were good with me." "And he said that he's a father for 14 kids, 7 boys and 7 girls and he's working here in Kuwait for a long time and the doctor's says from him that he will be find soon and they also says that they cut a little bit from his stomach and they found three bullets inside his body and now everything is OK."

Although Syrians are not always known to be allies of the United States, there's a very reasonable assumption that someplace in the world today, there is one father of 14 children who thinks of us daily, and is praising two American soldiers who did their job well.

Chapter 9

While the American civilian drivers were immediately aware that their personal safety rested in the Coalition soldiers who escorted the convoys, other sub-contract drivers from various countries in the Middle East continued to lose contact with the reality that their lives, too, depended on the military.

On September 1, 2003, I sat with friends from the Kuwaiti Army at the border of Iraq. There were, at the time, two roads that were available for travel between the two countries. They were approximately a mile apart, and whereas one road was for the use of civilian traffic between the two countries, the second was for the dedicated use of military and expatriate convoys. Convoys from TCN countries, which were under the security of our own military, would also use the military access.

As we sat, drinking hot tea, a lone figure could be seen as he walked the barren stretch leading back to Kuwait. He eventually arrived at the gate and met with one of the English-speaking interpreters.

Javed Ahmed Mohammad, a Pakistani driver, related the all-too-familiar story. He and another Pakistani driver had been driving toward Baghdad when the two decided to make better time by leaving the safety of their convoy. Approximately 20 miles from the border a small pickup truck that was occupied by five males drove beside the two trucks and motioned for the drivers to stop. When Mohammad failed to stop, the insurgents began their customary firing of AK-47s. The end result was that Javed pulled to the side of the roadway and his life was spared; however, his load of supplies and tractor trailer were taken by the insurgents. The Pakistani driver who was in the following vehicle was shot and left motionless on the side of the road. His truck was also taken by the terrorists.

When I interviewed Javed Mohammad it became obvious that his own attackers were the same people who had attacked other trucks on August 29, 2003, at the same time and location. In the previous attack, two other unescorted trucks that were operated by TCN drivers had been taken and four drivers were still missing.

On September 3, 2003, I was telephonically contacted by an English-speaking Kuwaiti who identified himself as a friend of Javed Mohammed. The caller related that the Pakistani owner of the truck that Mohammed had been driving had been contacted by the insurgents who offered to return the truck for $8,000 in U.S. currency. Ironically, the insurgents advised that they were offering the truck back at a reduced rate since the owner was of Pakistani descent and not from Kuwait. The demand for ransom had been made from Javed's personal cell phone that was left inside the truck when it was hijacked.

Javed's Kuwaiti friend advised me that the insurgents had instructed Javed to bring the money that afternoon to the Kuwait border where he would be met and the truck would be turned over after the appropriate ransom was paid.

I immediately contacted the military police at NAVISTAR and informed them that the murderers intended on coming to the border to receive payment for the truck. I was politely advised by the M.P. captain that the issue was basically above his pay grade. I was put in contact with the Army Criminal Investigations Division at Camp Arifjan in Kuwait. My response from C.I.D. was that they didn't want to risk the lives of Army personnel in attempting an apprehension. Although I politely informed the C.I.D. personnel that their proactive approach to resolving the problem could save military lives in the future, I soon realized I was not going to obtain cooperation.

Later that afternoon Javed returned to the Kuwait/Iraq border, accompanied by a well-dressed Pakistani male who was carrying a briefcase. They made a cellular phone call and a short time later a bright orange-colored taxi approached the border from inside Iraq. A few minutes later a Jeep utility vehicle, white, with a red stripe approached the border. I then watched in amazement as a ransom payment was made and within minutes Javed's truck was driven up to the border. Javed entered his truck and drove it across the border into Kuwait. My only satisfaction was in taking photographs as the ransom was exchanged for the 18-wheeler.

Ironically, the next day the bright orange taxi returned to the border with a large wooden box tied to the roof. The lone driver related that he'd "found" the body of a truck driver approximately 20 miles from the Kuwait border. The taxi driver expressed interest in being paid a reward for locating and returning the body of the unknown driver.

I checked the passport that accompanied the remains of a male who was believed to be of Pakistani descent. He wasn't a documented driver for KBR or any of our subsidiaries. When I informed the Kuwait Border Patrol that the remains didn't belong to KBR, they refused to let the body into their country because the decedent wasn't in possession of a visa.

For three days the taxi returned to the border in hopes of getting someone to take possession of the body and pay a reward for its return. The Kuwaitis were adamant in their refusal to accept a body which undoubtedly had originally left Kuwait in a convoy. The rapidly decaying body must have eventually been discarded by the

Good Samaritan because the odor from the body was beyond description.

Within days, whenever a truck was taken by the insurgents, they would also take the cell phone belonging to the driver so they could call and make demands for ransom of the truck.

In just a relatively few days I'd seen the birth of a new cottage industry in Iraq: the hijacking of trucks by insurgents and the payment of ransom for the release of the truck. Meanwhile, the insurgents took whatever supplies may be inside the trailer for whatever purpose they chose, would strip the vehicle of all but the bare essentials to keep it running, and would collect their reward for what they'd taken in the first place.

Chapter 10

On September 30, 2003, I had the occasion to be talking with one of the Kuwait Border Security guards when I disclosed that I'd written two books that had been published in the United States. The fact that I was a retired police detective, former elected mayor of a small American city, or had worked as a bodyguard for DuPont Company, a major corporation, meant nothing to my host. You can rest assured that the fact I was at that time employed by Halliburton meant even less.

Before the conversation had ended, my friend on the border contacted his superiors to advise them that the new security man, Elmer, was a writer. Suddenly, or though it seemed, I was receiving credit for penning two books, even though my family and a few close friends had been my only readership. My friend at the border informed me that his commander wanted me to come to his office immediately.

Within an hour I was in the office of Colonel Leyad T. Abdul Salam, Commander of the Kuwaiti Department of Border Patrol and Coast Guard. I had not neglected to take a couple of my first book, *Overkill- A Detective's Story*, as a gift for the Colonel.

While sitting in the Colonel's office and drinking hot tea, or chai as it was better known, I realized that I was being afforded a courtesy that had never been extended to most of the higher-ranking military personnel in the area, and definitely not to any representatives from Halliburton or KBR. It was an opportunity!

We spent a considerable period of time just socializing before getting down to any business at hand. Actually, I had walked into his office with no business at hand, yet had decided in our conversation that Colonel Salam might be an excellent resource for KBR.

Firstly, I was advised that I would be receiving increased support from the border guards in being notified of problems that might occur. The Colonel informed me that his subordinates would contact me by cellular phone should something occur that American security needed to be aware of. This was indeed progress because in the past, a driver from some small country could return to the border, advise he had a body of a driver who'd been found along the roadway, and be sent on his way toward Kuwait with no reporting of the recovered body ever being made.

Colonel Salam also advised me that he would instruct his border patrol units that whenever a supply transporter returned to Kuwait without their escort, then the Kuwait Government would prohibit them from entering the country. We had to fine-tune that commitment as I could just imagine a hundred or more trucks, operated by TCNs, being relegated to remain in Iraq while vandals or insurgents methodically disassembled their tractor and trailers. We compromised at letting the trucks back into Kuwait, but making them remain parked at the border for an indefinite period for disciplinary reasons.

The only thing the Colonel asked in return was whether or not I could obtain a couple of sets of night-vision glasses that his personnel at the border could utilize while performing their assignments. I thought this was a very workable exchange, yet later learned from a senior KBR manager that it appeared to be too closely related to a bribe.

Our agreement lasted just about long enough for me to inform the Colonel that obtaining the night-vision equipment wasn't going to be possible. At least one positive result from the meeting was increased cooperation between KBR Security and the Kuwait Department of Border Patrol and Coast Guard.

For the most part, relations with the Kuwait border personnel went smoothly most of the time. Yet sometimes, for no apparent reason, the Kuwait Armed Forces would flex their muscle and decide to remind the Americans that Kuwait was its own boss.

One such incident was in August 2003 when Joe Brown, my security manager, contacted me by phone and advised me to get an interpreter to the border.

On arrival at the border crossing I learned that the Safwan Bypass, a small stretch of road that had been dedicated to the use of our American supply movements, had been closed to all but military personnel, in uniform, and who were occupying military vehicles. This effectively meant that supply movements that were manned by American civilian employees of KBR would not be allowed to cross the border. The issue became more perplexing when we learned that many of our drivers and trucks were being confined to a less than friendly area on the Iraq side of the crossing.

After several hours the situation was resolved, or resolved itself, and our drivers were allowed back to the safety of Kuwait.

Although we were never able to ascertain who'd given the order to restrict our convoy movements, I do know that the incident reached and was resolved by the United States Embassy in Kuwait.

My hat went off to Captain Moran when he informed the Kuwait border officials that he was bringing his troops across the border of Kuwait, and challenged any Kuwaiti to stand in his way. The American soldiers and KBR drivers who were across the border were granted immediate access into Kuwait.

Chapter 11

Throughout my first several weeks working in the Middle East I was able to maintain phone and internet contact with family and friends who remained in the U.S. They all wondered what life was "really" like in a hostile environment. What could I say that would appease their desire for the real story?

Upon arrival in Kuwait I spent approximately two hours in a hot tent while waiting to be processed into the country. That evening I was in a luxury resort on the Persian Gulf where I remained for several weeks. The food was excellent and thanks to the United States Department of Defense I drove a new sport-utility vehicle. Did I mention the service staff that cleaned my room on an almost daily basis?

In short, life was good. Kuwait and the hospitality of her people were constantly present.

My transfer to APOD at the Kuwaiti airport was also a refreshing change. Yes, I had to forego the luxury resort at Kalifa, and found myself sleeping in an eight-man tent. Even then the tents were air-conditioned, the dining facility was mere steps away, and there was never a shortage of hot water or toilet facilities.

While at APOD I was the sole security coordinator and with the exception of handling the William Dover shooting and witnessing the transfer of some of the remains of our American soldiers, APOD provided a great respite.

Whenever I began to feel a bit homesick, I'd just jump into my SUV and drive to the main terminal of the airport for a haircut or a dinner of Kentucky Fried Chicken.

My introduction to reality came when I was transferred to Camp Udairi, which was located away from the bright lights of Kuwait and nestled in the desert area nearer the border with Iraq. My daily trips to "Bubba's" were not only tedious, they represented new dangers that I hadn't yet experienced. There were hundreds of areas along the deserted road where insurgents could gain entry from Iraq and wait for an unsuspecting potential victim. Sand storms were the norm where visibility was nonexistent, and the threat of a head-on collision on narrow roads was always a possibility and on some occasions, a guarantee. Additionally, by being closer to the war zone I began to see and appreciate the reality of war and the sanctity of life.

It was while making the trips between Udairi and the border that I experienced my first of what would be many frightening moments in my service as an expatriate.

On one occasion, while returning to Udairi late at night, I observed the headlights of a vehicle that was overturned in the desert. I realized the potential of a possible attack from a staged accident, but also knew my obligation of ensuring that someone wasn't trapped inside the vehicle. I attempted to telephone the KBR Command Center at Camp Arifjan by cellular phone. There was no service! I then drove into the desert and drove in a large circle around the wrecked vehicle to ascertain if there were footprints that would indicate if someone had abandoned the vehicle after the accident. There were no prints that I could see. At this point I realized that someone could likely be inside the vehicle, but also recognized the potential of being set up for death.

Since KBR policy prohibited their security personnel from being armed, I was not armed with anything other than a pocket knife for defense.

Luckily, an American convoy passed and I was able to flag them down. Our American soldiers, with their weapons at the ready, checked the accident and although blood indicated someone had been injured in the accident, they had somehow managed to crawl from the remnants of the vehicle and disappear into the night.

The wrecked vehicle remained for several days as a reminder to me of the potential for being injured in the remote area.

The road that led to Camp Udairi was also known as the "Highway of Death," dating from the Gulf War when hundreds of Iraqis were killed as they attempted to return to their country after attacking Kuwait. There were remains of hundreds of Iraq's military trucks that remained destroyed when the remnants of the Iraqi Army had attempted to return to Iraq. The "Highway of Death" in Kuwait should not be confused with the highway of the same name that runs from the Green Zone in Baghdad to the Baghdad International Airport. The airport road at BIAP is also known as the "Purple Heart Highway."

Chapter 12

September 9, 2003, was a busy day for vandals and insurgents inside Southern Iraq.

At 10:15 AM a convoy returned from delivering supplies in Iraq. While approaching the border, KBR Convoy Commander Ernest Mobley reported that his trucks were attacked by vandals who were throwing rocks at the passing trucks. When the convoy arrived at the Kuwait entrance, we determined that eight KBR trucks had received damage from thrown rocks that would necessitate replacement of windshields in all of the vehicles.

At 12:00 PM a second convoy that was led by KBR Convoy Commander Mike Fieto crossed the border and reported that six of the windshields in that convoy had been broken.

By 6:00 PM that evening unknown vandals strung barbed wire across the roadway within eyesight of the border.

What is amazing about the literally hundreds of windshield and passenger windows that were broken by rocks, these same drivers were encountering random gun fire, IEDs, and the frequent attempts by insurgents to stop the convoys.

No one will ever fully understand the dangers that American expatriates faced while working as convoy drivers in Iraq.

Because of the frequency of attacks on our convoys during the months of August and September 2003 I began researching all reports that had been submitted by me, Steve Pulley, and other security coordinators who were charged with interviewing victims of the attacks. A pattern began to emerge. Many of these attacks were committed against Third World drivers who were under subcontract to KBR. Many attacks were against U.S. civilians whose most important dream was to have a better life from the high salaries they were being paid.

- Wednesday appeared to be the day of choice for attacks.
- Attacks were committed between 10:00 AM and 2:00 PM.
- The first attacks were committed approximately 25-30 kilometers from the Kuwait border, but were progressing to the area of the first bridge north of Safwan.
- One crime was reported 80 kilometers from the Kuwait border, but ransom payment for the truck was made at Safwan, a short distance from the Kuwait border.
- Suspects were armed with handguns and AK-47s during every attack.
- Since the first reported attack, the numbers of suspects and vehicles that were involved had increased. It was also becoming more apparent that the insurgents were utilizing better planning and more firepower from their weapons of choice.
- Of all the reported crimes, six involved a red-in-color GMC vehicle or an older-model Chevrolet that was painted black or dark green. A white-in-color minibus and a white-in-color Jeep Cherokee had also been used during attacks.
- All attacking vehicles will have 5-6 Iraqi males inside.
- Most attacks were against TCN drivers who had left the security of military escort.

• The suspects frequently attacked TCN drivers where the drivers were in a movement of 1-9 trucks.

• Many attacks began with children throwing rocks at the traveling vehicles. When there was no military intervention, it was apparently assumed the drivers were traveling without security and attack conditions were more favorable.

During the first week of September 2003 a civilian employee of Halliburton's subsidiary, KBR, Vernon Gaston was fatally shot while driving in an escorted convoy in Baghdad. That victim, from the Texas area, was transporting mail when he was killed. The killing brought to mind the shooting death of another KBR employee during the month of August who had also been transporting mail for civilian and coalition troops. At the time I terminated my employment with KBR, these two employees who were carrying mail to our soldiers and expatriates had been killed during terrorist attacks.

During the middle of September 2003 I returned to Tampa, Florida, for my first vacation. While at home, I received an e-mail from my manager, Joe Brown.

Hey Buddy

I hope your R&R has been good. I remember you talking some time ago about wishing you could get to the Turkish border as you speak the language. Looks as if your wish is going to be granted as it looks like I am going to need you and Jason Mask at the Turkish border as we will be pushing approximately 20,000 convoys from there. Will fill you in on it when you get back over here.

Enjoy the rest of your R&R.
Joe

I spent the rest of my vacation on cloud nine. The Turkish border had been closed by the Turks during the war, but now the "Turks" had granted permission for fuel shipments between Turkey and Iraq to resume. The problem was, there were 20,000 fuel trucks backed up on the Turkish side, and no one was getting the trucks into Iraq where the supplies were desperately needed.

Also, while on my vacation back in the U.S., I had the opportunity to spend countless hours watching the news channels for stories related to Iraq. Although I'd heard comments on many occasions that linked Halliburton Corporation to the Vice President of the United States, Dick Cheney, for some reason I began to take offense. Primarily, I realized then, as I do now, that Halliburton never questioned the political affiliation of any expatriates that were hired for the reconstruction efforts of Iraq. I knew from hundreds of conversations with fellow employees in Kuwait and the Iraqi border that many of my colleagues were Democrats. It seemed strange that the Democratic Party chose to make such an issue out of the fact that our Vice President had at one time been the Chairman of the Board of Halliburton. This would not be the last time that I would resent the politicizing of Iraq.

Chapter 13

I returned to Kuwait sometime around the first week of October 2003. My friend Joe Brown met me inside the terminal when I arrived after clearing through customs processing.

Joe informed me that the travel plans were for me to fly on a military C-130 to Baghdad, along with Jason Mask, who would be supervising the transportation efforts of getting fuel into Iraq from Turkey. We would be assigned vehicles in Baghdad and proceed, via convoy, to Mosul, Iraq, then on to the Turkish border.

Two days later I returned to Kuwait International Airport and proceeded to the military side of the airfield. We were briefed by military personnel and learned that from the time of our departure we'd be required to wear protective Kevlar vests and Kevlar helmets. Thanks to the efforts of Joe Brown, he'd obtained a military vest for me that would provide more protection that the vests that were traditionally issued by KBR.

The flight into Baghdad was uneventful until our pilot announced that we were over Baghdad and would be landing in minutes. I looked out the window of the C-130 and noted that we seemed to be too high to expect a quick landing. Boy was I wrong. Unknown to me, planes landing at Baghdad International Airport were frequent targets of insurgents and landing at the airport was quite dangerous. Our pilots made what was later referred to as a "corkscrew" landing.

From our high altitude the plane was suddenly spiraling toward the ground, making quick circles in the air as we reduced altitude, but increased speed. My initial impulse was that we were crashing; however, I did note one of the crew members as he casually looked out the window of the plane. After a minute or so until we suddenly straightened out and after a short guide path, we landed safely.

The landing was symbolic for two reasons. First, I was finally in Iraq, and secondly, I was now earning an additional 55 percent on my weekly salary.

I would spend one night in the infamous "Green" Zone of Baghdad. After being transported from the airport into Baghdad, via the Purple Heart Highway, we had dinner in an ornate dining hall that was strategically placed in the ballroom of one of Saddam's palaces. The signs of opulence were everywhere. Adjacent to the palace was a huge, Olympic-size pool where hundreds of our civilians and military were enjoying an afternoon swim.

Jason Mask and I wouldn't have time for recreational activities. Jason was busy meeting with the managers of the Turkish border fuel team while I received security briefings on what to expect while traveling via convoy to the Turkish border.

It was also while in the Green Zone that we met Charles Breckenridge, a retired military officer who would be the lead manager on our mission. Breckenridge had a personal philosophy that he lived by. "Mission First and Personnel Always" was his motto.

I also learned that our small team of civilians would be billeted with Captain Hosler of the U.S. Army, 632nd MCT group at the Ibrahim Khaleel Customs Facility in Zakho, Iraq. I learned that our group would work with Kurdish military in inspecting the fuel shipments, getting fuel trucks out of Turkey where there was a serious backup of hundreds of loaded fuel tankers, and that members of the 632nd MCT would provide security escorts for the trucks into Mosul, Iraq. It all seemed so cut and dried. It would become a nightmare.

The following morning, Jason and I were taken to a secure area where we were each issued a brand-new Ford Excursion. We had just enough time to get the SUVs washed before it was time to depart.

As was customary with all convoy travel in Iraq, we met with members of the Army escort units who provided us with their customary briefing. We were told that if our convoy was attacked, the military plans were to engage the enemy and we would not proceed further until all insurgents had been eliminated. The officer in charge of the detail further informed us that on the first leg of our travel we'd be going to Camp Anaconda in Balad, Iraq. This would be around 70 miles travel during the first part of the journey. We were also informed of several locations along the way that were hot beds of terrorists.

My vehicle, followed by Jason in his new Excursion, would be the third and fourth vehicles in line. We would be following a military Humvee that was equipped with a .30-caliber machine gun, and followed by a ton-and-a-half truck that would be equipped with a .50-caliber machine gun.

Our specific instructions were not to allow any civilian vehicles, under any conditions, to break into our convoy.

Jason Mask was turning out to be a great partner to work with. By trade, he was a former cross-country driver of 18-wheelers who had been hired as the war ended to drive supplies into Iraq. He'd obviously showed such promise that he was quickly promoted and was now going to the Turkish border as a transportation logistics coordinator. Since Jason had traveled these same roads in convoys, he knew what to expect and was a terrific mentor to me.

By the time we reached Camp Anaconda, Jason had begun his nonstop rhetoric in kidding me about whether or not my AARP card would be recognized if my Ford SUV was disabled by an improvised explosive device.

We made it to Camp Anaconda well before dark and were met by my friend Steve Pulley, who had recently been assigned to work as a security coordinator at that base. We would spend the night at Anaconda before proceeding to Tikrit and Mosul the following day.

Thankfully, Steve not only showed us where we'd be sleeping that night, he also pointed out the bunkers we should go to when mortars were fired at the camp. We'd finished dinner and were preparing to get some rest when we heard and felt the tremendous explosion of a mortar as it landed somewhere in the camp. For a couple of hours we sat inside our bunkers and waited for the next explosion that never came. There was a bright side to the incident. Since Jason and I had completed our required 12 hours of work for the day, our time spent in the bunker was billable as overtime.

The following morning, Pulley bid us farewell as our convoy departed for Tikrit, the hometown of Saddam Hussein.

Unfortunately, we arrived too late in Tikrit to catch another convoy that would be heading to Mosul. We stayed overnight and fought the dust storms that were so prevalent in the area.

The following morning we were at the departure area bright and early. During our briefing by the military we were informed that if the convoy was attacked, we'd continue on our journey and there would be no engagement of the enemy.

While proceeding to Mosul we were going through the town of Tikrit when the convoy slowed to a crawl and then we picked up speed. As we proceeded through the town there was a noticeable presence of American soldiers who were in various stages of combat readiness. Two fuel trucks were burning beside the road.

It would not be before we arrived at the airbase in Mosul, Iraq, when we would learn that our convoy had been attacked and several insurgents had been killed. Ironically, our convoy was so long that Jason and I, who were at the front of the convoy, didn't know an attack was ongoing.

Once we arrived in Mosul we were met by other security coordinators from KBR who had arranged a military escort to take us on to the Turkish border. Because it was getting dark and KBR personnel aren't allowed to travel at night, we exceeded 70-80 miles an hour to get to the border before darkness.

Considering the high risks involving driving through Mosul, the high speeds were very welcome to us all.

Chapter 14

On October 9, 2003, I e-mailed my first report to John Davis, who had replaced Joe Brown as the next link in my chain of command since I was no longer in Kuwait. Perhaps I should refer to John as the "missing link." John worked out of the Corporate Security office in Baghdad. (I will also add that John Davis is an alias I've given to this individual. Under his true name, or alias, I will always consider him a total idiot.)

> John
> I met with Captain Hosler, the on-scene commander for Habur Crossing this afternoon and attended the daily security briefing this evening. The captain is aware that my SF 86 is still in the process and has no problem with my attending the daily security briefings. These

are conducted at 2000 hours daily. The captain has also placed his personal interpreter at our disposal which has already been of value.

There are no current "known" threats and I will be immediately notified of any changes.

We crossed the border today with the interpreter and began necessary introductions. Our visit was well received and we will be returning tomorrow. There will undoubtedly be obstacles as the Turks view the Kurdish residents as their enemy. I've distanced myself as much as practical from this issue. Turkish representatives indicated that there's a KBR "employee" who is currently working on their side of the border. It's my suspicion that this individual may be an employee of one of the subcontractors for KBR who is using the clout of the KBR name to get his own trucks across the border. This matter will be further investigated to ensure we receive the ultimate benefit of any contacts this individual might have on the Turkish side.

Charles Breckenridge provided an excellent resource for us in his selection of Charley Lecara from I.T. Charley assisted the Kurdish Customs office with restoring their own computer to service, thus gaining cooperation in locating suitable office locations. Our own computer system should be ready upon approval for office selection. The office issue is being handled between Jason and Breckenridge since security can function out of whatever location is convenient for the transportation side of this project.

Realizing that personnel safety is one of your primary concerns, I can only state that I feel extremely comfortable with existing security and know that although potential threats are never totally eliminated, they have been reduced to an acceptable level. Since our arrival, there has not been a moment when KBR personnel have been outside the sight and protection of Kurdish protective forces.

I will keep you updated as we progress.

Elmer

The following night I sent my first e-mail to my wife, Donna, from my new assignment in Zakho, Iraq. I will honor the wishes of the Kurds by referring to the area as the country of Kurdistan.

Hi Honey

Just finished my first full day in the border area. I guess I could sum it up by saying I just love this assignment.

The Kurds are a great people. I'm finding them to be friendly, helpful, great senses of humor, and loyal. They've sure looked out for me since my arrival last night.

I'm located by a river that sits at the foot of a fairly big mountain. We're in the Kurdish Customs site and there's a restaurant right next door to where we stay. Can't say too much for the sleeping accommodations but am sure we will rectify that. After all, KBR wants us to have everything we need.

Had our first meeting this morning but just relaxed and looked around for the first day. Will probably do the same tomorrow.

I feel as safe as any place I could be. There are so many Kurdish soldiers and intelligence people who love Americans and are dedicated to keeping us safe.

On the top of my building, at any given time, are Iraqis who were caught trying to get across the border into Turkey. Most of them have been caught on the Turkish side and they're picked up by a bus and brought to our roof top. Don't know how long they stay there.

The work here is going to be extremely challenging, but, my friend, Jason, and I are up for the task. This is the kind of location where I wouldn't mind just finishing out the contract.

As I mentioned on the phone, the trip up here was convincing in assuring me that all's not right in the world. There were a couple of really scary moments but all turned out well, and safe.

On October 12, 2003, Muric Khalil, a Turkish national, was returning to the border after offloading a shipment of diesel fuel to Mosul. Khalil chose to return to the border without waiting for an escort team from 632nd MCT.

While proceeding north on the main supply route, in the area of Filfil, Iraq, a vehicle pulled alongside the victim's truck and several shots were fired that struck Khalil in the upper portion of his body. When the tanker stopped, Khalil was robbed of an undetermined amount of money and his truck was set on fire.

It wasn't until October 14 that I or the military became aware of the incident. The body of Muric Khalil had been taken back to Turkey without our knowledge. Mr. Khalil was the first KBR sub-contract driver from Turkey who lost his life after more than 50,000 fuel movements.

My own investigation revealed that the victim had showed poor judgment in leaving the security of the military, and traveling during the hours of darkness.

Perhaps the significance of the death of the Turkish driver was the knowledge that even though we were in an area that was normally considered safe, there's no place in Iraq where safety should be taken for granted. I met with Jason and the small team of civilians that we were accumulating and conducted a safety meeting.

As time progressed along the Turkish border, it was becoming more and more apparent that there wasn't a great need for a security coordinator at that location. Or, perhaps I was beginning to realize that the change of assignment had somewhat removed Joe Brown from his supervisory role over me and I was required to report to "higher" echelons out of Baghdad. In just a short time I realized that those individuals involved in the KBR security program inside the confines of Iraq were more difficult to work with and didn't have the faith in their subordinates that Joe Brown had.

Joe Brown had become a lifelong friend the day I met him in Kuwait. He was a former deputy sheriff from a county police department in Florida and like everyone else, he wanted to earn his pay during the reconstruction of Iraq, stay safe, and return safely to his family. Brown was somewhat quick tempered, but would listen to the suggestions of his personnel, carefully evaluate the content, and would make a reasoned and fair decision on how problems might be dealt with. I believe that Joe and I held a similar view that many of the day-to-day issues that faced KBR personnel were resultant of criminal activity more than a continuation of the war. In view of the fact that many of the security coordinators were former career military, the blend of former law enforcement personnel with former military personnel ensured that we had a stronger security department. Unfortunately, many of the managers in the higher echelons of security were strictly from a military background and had no regard for the expertise that a law enforcement career might provide. One thing that was becoming apparent was that Joe's authority was in Kuwait and I was dealing with issues occurring in Iraq.

On October 28, 2003, a Turkish driver, carrying fuel, crossed the Turkish border into the Ibrahim Khaleel Customs facility. A female soldier from the 632nd MCT climbed onto the running board of the truck to direct the driver to the marshalling area. Unfortunately, the driver misjudged the purpose of the 632nd and reached out the window, deliberately touching the soldier on her breast. The soldier used her training in defending herself by quickly, and somewhat forcibly subduing her assailant. The driver was immediately taken to the detention area of the customs facility where he was incarcerated.

Although the incident was by no means a laughing matter, I did choose the humorous aspect in submitting my report, which read in part:

> As 281 Turkish convoy drivers stood gathered in the morning chill of the Ibrahim Khaleel Customs Facility near Zakho, Iraq, the prisoner was escorted from the confines of his detention cell where he'd been incarcerated since the evening of October 28, 2003. The prisoner was escorted by Captain Michael Hosler, Commanding Officer of the 632nd MCT, who was accompanied by representatives of the Kurdish Customs Police, Pesh Merga, and the prisoner's own employer. The purpose of this meeting was simple! As part of a plea bargaining agreement, the prisoner, Yusuf Yildirim, publicly apologized for the sexual touching of a female United States soldier who had been assigned to assist Yildirim prior to his transporting supplies into Iraq.
>
> Following the public apology, the driver was ceremoniously escorted to his parked vehicle where he retrieved personal belongings. He was then taken to his employer's vehicle where he was privileged to travel one final trip across the Iraq/Turkish border where the newly unemployed Yusuf will have plenty of time to ponder on his sins and transgressions.
>
> Meanwhile, in Zakho, the "big wheels keep on turning" with a new driver behind the wheel.

What I didn't mention in my report of the incident was that the Turkish employer of Yusuf assured all concerned that once the driver had crossed back into Turkey, both of his legs would be broken to ensure he would know never to touch a member of the United States Army.

While assigned to the customs facility it became more difficult to maintain communications with my wife in Florida. Although I was assigned a satellite phone, I knew that the expense of using it was "cost prohibitive." Luckily, our e-mail system worked for the most part of the time. And, there were more serious problems that needed to be dealt with. The one shower that was shared by approximately 80 soldiers and civilians suddenly only delivered cold water. We knew we were in trouble when a local plumber arrived and his only tools were a pick axe and a monkey wrench. Thank "Allah" for Kurdish plumbers as we were only required to take cold showers for one day.

The month of October brought Ramadan, the religious period for the Moslem faith. Marshad, the owner of the restaurant that was frequently patronized by the American troops, continued to feed us during this holy period, but added a $1.00 surcharge that was donated to the local mosque. During the month of Ramadan, tempers were somewhat short since the practitioners of the Islamic faith couldn't eat, drink, smoke, or have sex during the day. The Turks did continue drinking their hot tea so I could "chill" in the truck yard and practice my Turkish.

It was during this time that we became aware that many of the fuel transport drivers were getting the processed fuel for their missions in Turkey, and then bringing the fuel across the border where the trucks would jump out of their convoy and offload fuel at one of various gas stations between the Turkish border and Mosul. This "black market" enterprise was becoming quite profitable to the drivers. An e-mail that I sent to my wife provided my philosophy about dealing with the problem.

It's been a fairly slow day. Seven of our truckies got caught downloading gasoline behind a restaurant. I have their passports on my desk but the "Siphoning Seven" haven't found their thieving little way to my office. Perhaps I should spray Ronson lighter fluid on their little testicles, light a small "bomb," and just get the punishment over with. Then we'll give them a fair trial. Yes, working in Zakho is all about attitudes.

Although I joked about the issue, it was a continual problem with getting good fuel back into the country where it would be used by both Coalition forces as well as finding its way back into the general population.

On countless occasions we became aware that some of the Turkish drivers would fill their trucks with processed fuel in Turkey, then sell most of it before reaching Iraq. These drivers would then replenish their tankers with crude, not processed oil before offloading the contents at a military distribution center. This was yet another reason why there were incentives to distance one's self from the protective military escort teams.

On one occasion we apprehended a 16-year-old who was concealed on a fuel tanker. During questioning, he stated that he had attempted to enter Iraq with the goal of committing a Jihad against American soldiers.

Chapter 15

In an e-mail to Donna on October 26, 2003, my daily e-mail identified some serious issues that had been addressed by the military.

The nightly security meeting brought some real serious "issues" to the front burner. It seems that some of the soldiers are going through the Meals Ready to Eat (M.R.E.s) and taking out their favorite meals. This means that all that's left are the vegetarian meals and since the Captain isn't getting the Salisbury Steak Meal, complete with the oatmeal cookie, he's one pissed-off dude. It was a scene out of the Caine Mutiny movie when those strawberries were missing.

Oh, we did get one hot meal last night that was sent by convoy from Mosul to our border. They sent chili and turkey loaf. We also had our traditional carrots to round out the exquisite cuisine. Northing changes in the military. Somewhere, there's a military dietician who sits up at night coming up with the following day's ala carte meal.

It's amazing how life can be going so smoothly and something occurs that has a life-changing effect. While I was enjoying the e-mails going on between me and family in the United States, problems were about to surface which would test my own moral obligations and personal integrity. It would also convince me that Halliburton, and its subsidiary KBR just might not be the company that I wanted to remain associated with.

Chapter 16

On October 31, 2003, Jason Mask approached me with what he perceived as a pending problem. I knew that Jason wasn't prone to overreacting in any situation; therefore, anything he brought up of a serious nature was something I would pay close attention to. My e-mail that was immediately sent to John Davis in Baghdad related the problem.

John

Several incidents of a suspicious nature have occurred here at the border which convinces me that KBR requires the presence of armed security to assist in safeguarding our personnel.

On today's date, 10-31-2003, two suspicious males were observed loitering in the hallway outside the KBR, MCT office. Jason Mask reported that one subject walked by the office and began glaring in the window for a couple of minutes. He then walked away and within moments, a second subject arrived and repeated the process. Jason watched them and noted that once outside the building, the two were conferring with each other. This same pattern has been noted with others who walk the accessible hallway outside our office and although the purpose could be out of curiosity, I feel a proactive approach is of utmost importance.

A second item of concern is the fact that we're adjacent to the United Nations offices for the Zakho area. With the ongoing problems that the UN is experiencing, their personnel are frequently away from that office. This means that Turkish drivers who don't find them available are becoming more aggressive toward my group by linking our dual purposes and functions as one.

Our local intelligence advises us that if Turkey sends their military to assist as a member of the Coalition Forces, there could be a potential for terrorist acts in this immediate area. By being on the border we're exposed to "anyone" who might enter Iraq from Turkey.

I have discussed the issue of additional security with upper management from the border patrol. Their responses have been positive to the extent that with money, it can be accomplished. My concern is that we would be paying border security for someone who would be a security "generalist" when I feel a "specialist" is more appropriate for the safeguarding of my personnel.

Our contacts with U.S. Military Intelligence previously introduced us to an excellent contact who speaks Arabic, Turkish, and English. His background is in operational intelligence and he's affiliated with the Pesh. His presence would open a better dialogue with out drivers and would also serve to provide personal protection to KBR personnel who could be in harm's way. This individual would be armed and is acceptable to our hosts, the border security department.

"The cost to obtain the services of a security man is $350.00 per month, and I would assign him to the hours when personnel are in the office to ensure this location receives the necessary security that is afforded by Customs to other areas of the complex.

For your information, I've also scheduled a meeting with our personnel to emphasize their need to make themselves less visible as targets for potential threats.

Elmer

The response from John Davis was a clear indication to me that my recommendation had fallen on deaf ears. His response was sent on 10-31-2006 at 5:01 PM.

Elmer
This sound serious, but we do have some options. Are you co-located with the U.S. Military MCT personnel or has something changed here that I'm unaware of? Earlier, you stated that "I don't see anything other than an extremely dire emergency where we wouldn't be under the protective umbrella of the military."

While assigned to the Turkey project I was able to obtain armed guards due to the fact that the U.S. Army was locked down on Turkish bases. Two things played in our favor, Turks would not let U.S. Army personnel off their base and initially, they would not allow us on.

The difference here is that you should have U.S. Military personnel with you. Armed guards will take management's and corporate approval. Recommend you conduct a security assessment of the area and explain why the U.S. Military cannot or will not provide you suitable force protection. Management requires this because our first approach will be to the U.S. Army and corporate for approval.

John Davis (Security)

Upon receipt of John Davis's response I will candidly admit that I was fuming. My suggestion had been made because a KBR employee had presented what he felt was a security issue, I had evaluated the content of Jason's concerns, and had acted in what I felt was in the best interest of the personnel who depended on me for ensuring they had adequate security.

October 31, 2003, was actually a day of good will and bad will for me. The military group I worked with at the Turkish border was from the State of Nebraska. During my conversations with the Nebraska "team" several of them had mentioned that they would love to have an Omaha steak. It seemed like a perfect opportunity for me to show my appreciation for the protection they were providing for me, and the personnel I worked with. As it turns out, getting an American steak in a foreign company is not an easy thing to do. My e-mail to Julie Davis, Customer Care Department of Omaha Steaks in Omaha, Nebraska, had good intentions, but no success.

Dear Customer Service Department

I'm a civilian contractor employed by the Department of Defense and currently stationed with Nebraska U.S. Army personnel in Zakho, Iraq, which is approximately ten miles from Silopi, Turkey. I would guess there are an estimated 50 Nebraska personnel stationed at this border outpost that separates northern Iraq with southern Turkey.

During conversations with your military personnel, the one item that each man and woman "wishes" for is an Omaha steak. Can we work together to make that wish come true?

At the present time the soldiers at this outpost receive one "semi" hot meal a day that is brought from a military base approximately 80 miles away. Steak is not one of those meals. The remainder of their meals are M.R.E.'s (meals ready to eat) that are supplied by the U.S. Army.

I'm willing to pay the cost for providing a steak dinner to these personnel. In turn, I would hope that Omaha Steaks could figure out the logistics of getting them to "your" troops in this somewhat desolate area.

I'm sure that your marketing department could recoup what surely would be a "trying" experience with increased business if they choose to exploit their "good will" efforts to their troops.

"Please explore this request and respond when possible.

Elmer L. Snow, III
KBR Security Coordinator
Habur Crossing, Iraq-Turkey

The reply from Omaha Steak Company determined that they lost me as a customer for life.

Dear Mr. Snow

At this time we are not able to ship anything into Iraq, or any Middle Eastern country.

If I can be of further assistance, please feel free to contact us via e-mail, or if you prefer, call our Customer Care Specialists at 1-800-329-6500.

Sincerely
Julie Davis
Customer Care

Well, that idea had been shot down! Personally, I thought that Omaha Steaks would not pass up a great opportunity to gain public support by making every conceivable effort to feed their troops.

Meanwhile, my own internal war with Halliburton management was heating up.

I held my temper in check when I replied to John Davis at 6:45 PM on October 31, 2003.

> John
>
> Prior to my initiating my request I did explore options that I should have mentioned in my original e-mail.
>
> The military has 24-hour security at the MCT yard where we also have KBR personnel assigned on a 24/7 assignment. I feel comfortable with the safety of those personnel to the extent that we all know our work isn't without some risks.
>
> Our billeting is with our own military personnel. Again, I feel comfortable with that issue insofar as safety of personnel is concerned.
>
> Unfortunately, the protective umbrella doesn't extend to our office area. I discussed this with Captain Hosler of the 632nd MCT. Hosler feels, as I do, that by utilizing local security we would maintain a lower profile that would not be present if a uniformed soldier was posted at our office. A "local" would be able to blend into their surroundings and create less visibility. A local, who also speaks the native language, would not only hear passing conversation, they would also be able to interpret for us when the need arises. As you will recall, we previously requested the hiring of an interpreter, which was approved. In this situation, we could have both security and an interpreter at our office.
>
> Would I categorize my request as being made as a

"dire emergency"? No! I would only categorize it as a dire emergency if we did nothing and in hindsight suffered injury or loss to KBR personnel. It is for this reason that I made my recommendation.

Elmer "Corky" Snow
KBR Security Coordinator

During what was becoming a somewhat "mini battle" between John Davis and me, Charles "Scott" Breckenridge, the regional operations manager in Baghdad, sent me a somewhat comforting e-mail.

Corky
It hasn't always been pretty at this end. I think I've made a few more enemies.

You haven't said much, so when you speak, I'll listen. Let me know what you need and when you need it.

Keep in mind the "no blood no foul rule" is in effect.
Scott
Charles "Scott" Breckenridge
Regional Operations Manager

Despite the ongoing e-mail skirmish that was quickly turning into Gulf War II, other problems at the border seemed to indicate that there was an air of violence that was gaining a foothold in and around the Turkish border.

On November 11, 2003, a convoy departed from the border and proceeded toward Fulfil with a line of tankers that were carrying fuel. Approximately four miles north of the delivery site, the convoy was passed by an orange taxi that was occupied by Iraqi males.

The taxi pulled in front of the lead vehicle and suddenly the trunk of the taxi opened up. An Iraqi male began firing an AK-47 at the military escorts. One projectile struck a PFC Davis in the right ankle and sped out of the area.

This was the second attack that Sergeant Dewarren Gaddy of the 801st MSB, United States Army, had encountered in a week. Gaddy, who was serving as a convoy commander, was earning his salary.

Although the field of combat was heating up with the supply transportation, the war between me and John Davis was also taking a turn for the worse.

Davis must not have been too happy with my e-mail responses and directed that I contact him via satellite phone. When I contacted him, it was apparent that he had absolutely no idea of what my qualifications might be, whether or not I could be depended on, or anything other than he hadn't liked my original suggestion.

Following our phone conversation, I replied with e-mail to ensure there was a record of what our conversation had involved.

> Pursuant to our conversation, I wanted to reiterate a couple of issues that you weren't previously aware of.
>
> I have been in the Middle East region for six months, rather than three weeks. My previous assignment was at the Theater Transportation Movement (TTM) at the Kuwait/Iraqi border where I served as a security coordinator. I know that Joseph Brown, the transportation security manager in that area, will commend my performance in that position.
>
> I did serve honorably for three years in the 101st Airborne Division where I was assigned to the division M.P.s. I am a retired police detective and recipient of 42 official commendations which included "Police Officer of the Year," "Police Officer of the Month," and the "Chief's Award of Merit."
>
> I was employed for five years as a personal Protection Specialist for the Chairman of the Board and Board of Directors of DuPont Company in Delaware. Besides

the responsibility of protecting key executives, I was also assigned to collect, evaluate, and disseminate, intelligence information on terrorist groups who targeted corporate assets, including personnel and property.

Through attending high school in Ankara, Turkey, I learned to speak the Turkish language which has been invaluable in my current assignment where I interact with hundreds of Turkish drivers on a daily basis.

As a former elected mayor of a city in Delaware, I recognize the need to conduct business here with our client and hosts with the highest standards of integrity, respect, and performance, in meeting our corporate goals and objectives.

Elmer
Elmer "Corky" Snow
KBR Security

I realized that at this point my comments would mean nothing to John Davis. My only hope was to convince others in the e-mail chain that I was fully qualified and competent to make decisions that affected the safety and security of KBR personnel.

Davis did not extend the courtesy of a response. He had Gary Seideman, the security manager for the Mosul District, respond on November 11, 2003, at 6:17 PM.

Elmer
I spoke with John Davis today and you will be leaving the border tomorrow. You will be needed further south. I will arrive tomorrow with the new security coordinator and bring you back to Mosul where I'll get you on a convoy to Anaconda the following day.

Can you be ready with all your equipment when I arrive there about 10:00 AM? We will immediately come back on the Mosul run.

Gary
Gary Seideman
Security Manager, Mosul District

So that was it. I'd been transferred for fulfilling my role as a security coordinator. I decided that if any KBR personnel were to get injured or die, it wouldn't be because I hadn't stood on principle or in their best interest.

Chapter 17

November 6, 2003

Re: Resignation
Elmer L. Snow, III
KBR Security Coordinator
Zakho, Iraq

On October 31, 2003, I was approached by a KBR employee who expressed concerns of safety issues involving him, and personnel who are assigned to work for him.

The employee was concerned of a real potential of facing injury or death because of suspicious people he'd observed conducting a surveillance of the KBR office in Zakho, Iraq.

As the "on site" security coordinator I conducted an assessment of the matter, and based on my experience in the security field determined that the addition of one armed security specialist was necessary in order to reduce the threat facing KBR personnel to an acceptable level. I made that recommendation on October 31, 2003.

The response I received was instructions to "make the hard call when required and move the operation to another location." This opinion had already been considered by me, with input from involved personnel, and eliminated as too costly in terms of expense, loss of productivity, and the fact that it would in fact critically delay the mission which this "team" was mandated to accomplish in a short time. Through the benefit of "micro management" I was instructed to make a "hard suggestion" which, by the way, has led to my transfer to another site. This is a perfect example of "if you don't like the message, kill the messenger." In hindsight, I can only be thankful that I didn't make a request for two security personnel to augment existing security.

For your information, the security manager who conducted a security evaluation resultant from my recommendation advised me that he was suggesting that I remain on my current assignment. At least, this was the statement I was given.

I've elected to leave the employment of Halliburton as I'm a true believer that authority must be commensurate with responsibility and when an employee makes a recommendation that might save lives, how many recommendations can management expect to receive, and how many lives will ultimately be lost because their field personnel are afraid to make their thoughts and suggestions known?

Enclosed is an attachment from the Civil Affairs Office of the U.S. Army who is permanently assigned to Zakho. As you will note, our "client" sees the same threats as I saw, and basically makes the same recommendations that I made.

I thank all of you for affording me the opportunity to learn more about Halliburton and KBR through my six months of un-blemished service. As a stockholder of record, it's always gratifying to see where one's investment goes and how it's managed in the field.

My only suggestion would be to reduce the requirements for security personnel as there's no need to pay the higher salaries for experience, training, and qualifications if you're only going to transfer them when they utilize their skills.

Elmer L. Snow, III
KBR Security Coordinator

Two days later I left my friends and associates in Kurdistan and drove in a convoy to Mosul. I would spend the night in Mosul and depart on a C-130 military flight the following morning for Kuwait where I would get to see my friend, Joe Brown, once again.

During my final night in Iraq an incoming mortar hit near my living container, almost knocking me out of bed.

While returning to the safety and security of the United States I thought of the experience and vowed to write a book on my experience.

How would I know that before I'd have the opportunity to write my book, I'd be rehired by Halliburton to return to the Middle East?

Chapter 18

The 17-hour flight back to Florida provided ample time to review in my mind the past six months of my life.

I remembered the hundreds of soldiers I'd met and observed and took the moment to truly appreciate how great it is to be an American. I thought of the two staff sergeants, Green and Brockington, who had saved the life of a man who could, at one time, have been a sworn enemy of our country. I appreciated the fact that I was old enough to be the father or even a grandfather of these wonderful American troops and thought how proud their own families would be of them if they'd had the opportunity to view their efforts personally.

I thought of Joe Brown, my security manager, who had always trusted my instinct and had rewarded me by putting me in more responsible positions during every step of the way.

My thoughts would go to Steve Pulley, who had accepted the employment knowing he was going to be in a security specialist role, and had ended up being assigned in one troubled area after another. Steve remained in Iraq while his wife and two daughters remained in Texas where I'm sure they worried about his safety every day.

As I flew back to safety, I thought of the day at the Kuwait border when members of the Polish Coalition Forces had accidentally fired a round from their tank and had been required to stand at attention for hours because of the mistake. Chuckles came easy when I remembered that although all of those soldiers were dressed in battle fatigues, one lone soldier was wearing a pair of patent leather shoes that distinguished him from the entire company. Remembering their expressions, I knew how proud they had been to participate in the reconstruction project.

My thoughts returned to "Bubba's Truck Stop" at the Kuwait border where as a security coordinator I'd been asked to speak to employees on Improvised Explosive Devices. (IEDs), the devices that were so prevalent along supply routes that took so many lives of our military and expatriates. Unfortunately, when I was introduced to the large group of employees, the NAVISTAR camp manager advised the group that "Elmer is one of the most knowledgeable people we have in security and today he's going to talk about his experiences with IUDs." I can only pray that my readers know the difference in an IED and an IUD.

Thoughts and remembrances brought back one of the dinners our team had been served in the small restaurant in the customs facility at Zakho. One of our new employees pointed out a mouse to Marshad, the restaurant manager, as the mouse ran across the floor of the restaurant. Marshad had quickly replied, "It's good for them to be here, they eat the crumbs off the floor." Who can ever argue with logic?

A day later I landed at the Tampa International Airport and began a three-month period of relaxation, watching ongoing news about so many areas that I'd visited, even for a matter of hours, and enjoying the return to poor golf.

Chapter 19

The month was February, 2004. I'd enjoyed Christmas and New Year's at home in Sun City Center, Florida, and all seemed right with the world. Taxes had been submitted and I'd paid more in Federal taxes that at any time during my life. The salary earned in Iraq, although extremely profitable, had ensured that "Uncle Sam" received his fair share. Why should I have complained? I was helping my country in paying for the war effort.

Donna answered the phone and excitedly yelled that Joe Brown was calling from Kuwait. Although we'd exchanged e-mails since my return to Florida, I don't believe at that point I'd talked with Joe personally.

His message was short and sweet! "Hey, you lazy mother fucker, are you ready to come back over?"

"Not to work for John Davis," was my immediate reply.

Joe then assured me that John Davis was no longer on the KBR radar screen and he, Joe, was wanting me to return to work as a security coordinator and that my assignment would be a return to the Turkish border. The fact that the security coordinators had received a substantial raise was icing on the proverbial Halliburton cake. Joe also indicated that he expected approval for us to carry firearms soon.

I informed Joe I was ready to return whenever I could get processed.

Within days I was contacted by a human resource specialist in Houston who offered me the opportunity to rejoin KBR as a security coordinator. I was also advised that since I'd been away from the company for over three months, it would be necessary to go through the week of processing in Houston.

On March 10, 2004, I'd completed my rehire process after duplicating the procedure that I'd experienced in May 2003. Ironically, during my physical examination the doctor indicated that I was going to be turned down for employment because of a hearing deficiency. He quickly changed his mind when I informed him that I'd previously been working in Iraq, and if I had hearing issues it was because of the explosion of mortars and IEDs that I'd been exposed to. I was quickly granted an exception and approved for employment.

On March 10, 2004, I departed Houston International Airport for Dubai which had been established as the new debarkation site for American expatriates who were entering or leaving Iraq. I arrived in Dubai on March 11th where I would remain until departure for Kuwait on March 14, 2004. During my absence from the Middle East, KBR had located a beautiful "five star" hotel in Dubai that would serve as the location where all of our personnel would be processed from. As one who was involved in security operations, it did concern me that all of the Americans were staying in one location. Throughout my short stay I constantly identified areas of the complex where a car bomb could be detonated with disastrous effects.

Joe Brown and another security manager, Ray Simpson, were waiting inside the Kuwait International Airport when I arrived on March 14, 2004. It was a scene somewhat similar to the reuniting of three close relatives who hadn't seen each other for years. Our first stop on our agenda was dinner in Kuwait where Joe and Ray began a nonstop list of things that had occurred during my three-month absence. One concern that was very apparent was the fact that the violence in Iraq was increasing daily and the insurgents were better armed, better trained, and possessed a strong commitment to kill every American they could, as well as any sub-contract Third World drivers who were involved in the reconstruction program.

By the time that our first dinner was finished, I was intimately aware that the violence I'd witnessed during my first tour of duty in Iraq was a mere sampling of what to expect during my return assignment. The same problems we'd experienced with incoming mortars and roadside IEDs remained a continuing problem. In addition, suicide bombers were becoming more prevalent throughout Iraq.

Brown advised me that due to a shortage of suitable vehicles in Baghdad, this trip would mean my being assigned an SUV at Camp Arifjan in Kuwait, and the need to travel in military convoys from Kuwait to the Turkish border at Zakho, Iraq. This meant that in just a few days I would realize a dream I'd previously had. Since my previous tour of duty, it had been my desire to travel in a convoy from border to border in Iraq. This was going to become a reality, although Joe continually emphasized that the previously dangerous roadways had become increasingly hostile during my absence.

I remained in Kuwait until the morning of March 22, 2004. Brown had ample time to brief me, have a Chevrolet Suburban SUV issued to me, and upgrade my protective vests and helmet to ones that would afford me the best chance of survival during an attack.

At 5:30 AM on March 22, 2004, I left the security and beauty of the Khalifa and began my drive to NAVISTAR. When I arrived there I realized that despite its formal name, "Bubba's Truck Stop" remained "Bubba's."

By 9:20 AM I was in a military convoy, surrounded by .50-caliber machine guns, and traveling north into Iraq. Our first stop was at Camp Cedar where I would spend the night and get into another convoy the following morning. At 6:50 AM on March 23, 2004, my new convoy left Cedar, drove to another post, Scania, where we had lunch, then proceeded to the Baghdad International Airport where I would remain for another night. Because of my lack of knowledge surrounding BIAP, I decided to sleep in my SUV rather than be wandering the roads around the airport. Joe had emphasized that the area surrounding the Baghdad Airport had become notorious for terrorist attacks.

Our departure from BIAP was uneventful the next day and within a short time we arrived at Camp Anaconda near Balad. I remembered that during my last overnight stay at Anaconda, an incoming mortar had shattered the quietness of the night. This time there would be no problems and the following morning, on March 25, 2004, we left Camp Anaconda, arrived at Camp Speicher near Tikrit, and then drove on to Camp Diamondback in Mosul. My travel through the Tikrit area reminded me that this was the same area where my previous trip north had involved our being attacked by insurgents.

I spent the night in Mosul where I found Jason Mask, who had been promoted during my absence and assigned to Camp Diamondback. It was great spending time with Jason and listening to his little comments about wondering how AARP had allowed one of their star seniors to leave his retirement community.

Jason provided an excellent briefing regarding the final stages of my travel to the Turkish border where we'd served together. I was gratified to learn that the Kurdish forces remained committed to the safety and security of American personnel.

On March 26, 2004, I arrived, via convoy escort, to Kurdistan. I would have dinner at the little restaurant where Marshad, the owner, would inform me that the little mouse continued doing his job by keeping crumbs off the floor.

As a welcoming gift for my return, one of my friends from the Kurdish Pesh Merga presented me with a British Sterling, nine-millimeter submachine gun. Despite the fact that KBR personnel were still not authorized to carry weapons, my friend wanted the comfort of knowing that I would be better able to protect myself. I concealed my weapon within arm's reach until the date of my final departure from Iraq.

Ironically, since my departure, KBR now had several members of the Kurdish Intelligence forces who had been hired to ensure the safety of KBR personnel. I smiled when recalling that this issue had been exactly why I left the company months earlier.

Chapter 20

Returning to the Turkish border just didn't have the same excitement as when I'd been previously assigned there. Jason Mask was no longer on the site, which meant my good friend, confidante, and working partner was no longer available to harass me.

KBR had placed a new detail on the site who worked under a transportation manager, Brett Noble. Brett was pleasant to work with but was completely consumed with his assignment. There was no doubt as to why he was consumed. When I looked off of the roof of my residence, a line of fuel trucks were backed into Turkey as far as the eye could see.

Brett was an extremely religious young man and I believe I lost his true friendship when I stated that I felt the military should shoot the rock throwers who were creating so much damage to our trucks. Brett replied that they were only around 16 years of age. When I said "So?" It was then I think he decided I was just a heathen.

On a brighter side, security issues were almost non-existent, thanks to a new team from the military who took their assignment with total dedication.

On a personal level, I made out well. One of the reservists assigned to the border was John Sanford, who had been activated for the war. John was a lieutenant in the New York City Police Department, which meant we had many things in common. Working with Sanford was extremely nice because he saw issues as a soldier, and as a police detective. He was counting his days to get back to his police work and an expected promotion to captain.

I'd been back at the Turkish border for a couple of weeks with no problems occurring that required security. I spent most of my days creating attack scenarios in my mind and developing plans based on the particular problems I mentally created on how to survive. Despite the continual presence of Kurdish intelligence, I never overlooked the fact that a well-placed bomb among the hundreds of fuel trucks could leave the border compound as nothing more than a huge whole in the ground.

I maintained daily contact with either Joe Brown or Ray Simpson. Joe was spending more and more of his time in Baghdad where he could keep a closer overview of the hundreds of convoys and their increasing problems. He almost lost his life when a mortar was fired at the Sheraton Hotel he was staying in while working in Baghdad. I was relieved to learn that the mortar had landed on the tennis court at the hotel. Joe Brown just wasn't one who'd be found playing tennis but the information we received at the border was that the hit was too close for his comfort.

Although we were not experiencing any problems in the Zakho area, attacks on convoys from the Kuwait border all the way to Mosul were accelerating at mach speed. Scarcely a day would go by when news of another attack was passed through the corporate e-mail system. Ray Simpson worked many long hours in Kuwait as he assembled information for the security coordinators who were spread across Iraq.

As the attacks on convoys increased in the rest of the country, fuel shipments were significantly decreasing from Turkey. I wasn't surprised when Ray Simpson asked if I thought my services were really needed at the border. In all good conscience I wouldn't lie just to remain in somewhat of a safe haven. I suggested to Ray that I could be of assistance to Steve Pulley at Camp Anaconda, near Balad.

The following morning I received an e-mail from Joe advising me to pack up and start heading to Camp Anaconda via convoy. He also informed me that I would be teaming up with Shane Irwin, another security coordinator who'd been stationed at a base in Scania for a considerable period of time. I'd previously met Shane while working at Bubba's Truck Stop and had gotten him into the convoy that would take him to Scania. Irwin was a retired master sergeant from the 5th Special Forces Group of the U.S. Army. The rumor mill provided nothing but praise for Irwin and his ability to get the mission accomplished.

Two days later, with my British Sterling submachine gun nestled next to me, I left Zakho for the final time. I would enjoy one night in Mosul with Jason, who took the time to make me jealous by taking me on a tour of his office that was larger than life. That night I would lie in bed listening to the explosion of an incoming mortar and approximately ten minutes of continual machine-gun fire as the American soldiers responded to the attack.

Chapter 21

Camp Anaconda is located approximately 65 miles north of Baghdad and on the outskirts of the predominately Sunni town of Balad. The site is a former air base that was used by the Iraqi Air Force and was where Saddam Hussein had his dental work done. The base is strategically located for the convenience of convoys and coalition troops. With approximately 14 square miles inside the perimeter of the fences, there was ample space for numerous mortars and rocket propelled grenades (RPGs) to fly through the air and sometimes land with deadly consequences. An occasionally sniper round would be fired into the camp that added to the danger element.

When I arrived at Anaconda, Steve Pulley took me around the entire base and pointed out the various offices that I might need to go to. He also told me about "One Shot" Charley, who on a daily basis, without fail, would fire one mortar round into the camp. Pulley emphasized that "One Shot" normally struck around 4:00 PM, so his work could be identified more specifically than other randomly fired mortars that may hit the camp at any time.

There are many situations where fear can be an ally when working in a war zone. Controlled fear increases situational awareness and as long as one doesn't allow fear to escalate into panic, survival opportunity is increased.

On May 6th I sent an e-mail to Donna that provided details of the previous evening.

> The mortars last night proved to be surprisingly close. We took four of them and had to sit in the bunkers for an hour. I'll send a picture of the bunkers so you'll have an idea of the damage. One TCN (Third Country National) was slightly injured in one of the blasts, two SUVs were hit, and there were holes in two tents and one building.

On May 7th my e-mail home provided a continuation of the problems we were encountering from a very determined insurgent enemy.

> Billy Lewis and I are both really tired this morning. We just didn't get enough sleep and when you get up at 4:00 AM, it all catches up. We don't think the enemy fire last night was from "One Shot." He's usually off his aim and lately we've seen a much better degree in accuracy in the shooting. I guess that all total we must have taken around six mortars and perhaps one Rocket Propelled Grenade (R.P.G.) The first one had to go right over my SUV while Billy and I were heading back to

our rooms. It was still close enough to make my car swerve. Or, I made my car swerve when it landed. Although it sounded like it was exploding "on" the car, we were around 150 yards from where it impacted. That's still too close. Then, for three hours we sat in our bunkers while mosquitoes feasted on the sweaty bodies. All in all, it's been a hell of a week. One coworker killed, several mortars incoming, and terrible coffee at the dining facility. (DFAC) Ah, life is indeed good."

On May 8, 2004, a mortar was fired from outside the base and landed immediately adjacent to the KBR Transportation offices. A small passenger bus was passing along the gravel roadway when the mortar impacted with the ground. Pieces of metal and shrapnel exploded through the sides and windows of the bus. Several injuries were reported and I believe the bus driver demobilized back to the United States the very next morning. If the mortar had been a few feet closer, the report would have described the incident as catastrophic rather than extremely serious.

On May 9th we received intelligence reports that the Terrorist known as Al Sadr had met at a mosque with 3,000 of his most dedicated idiot followers. He offered $150.00 for each British soldier killed, $350.00 for a kidnapped British soldier, and told his followers that anyone capturing a female British soldier could keep her as his slave. This report created a considerable increase in our anger toward certain elements that were so intent on killing the good guys.

On May 10, 2004, Billy Lewis and I drove to the PX and decided to buy a couple of canvas chairs so our increasing period of time that was being spent inside our bunkers would be more of a quality time. In the least, it would be more comfortable than sitting on sharp rocks. We decided that the investment in chairs had been worthwhile when we received information that day that a convoy of TCNs had been attacked while arriving with supplies from Jordan. Our information indicated that at least 21 supply trucks had been completely decimated.

The remainder of the day was spent in cleaning our living quarters although "One Shot" did try to ruin our day by firing his customary one shot into the camp.

On May 11, 2004, fear turned into panic and lives were lost at Camp Anaconda.

As Steve Pulley, William "Billy" Lewis, and I sat in our office having coffee, there was no indication that severe problems were looming. A pattern of attacks that had been developing among the insurgents outside the base told us that we would probably have mortar attacks during the late afternoon.

We weren't expecting an early morning attack.

The impact of the first mortar hit with a deafening explosion that shook the foundation of our building. Our first instinct was to grab our Kevlar helmets and protective vests and begin to evacuate the building to seek shelter in one of the numerous bunkers that were nearby. While running from the door a second mortar landed 100 yards from the office and directly in the center of an encampment that housed several hundred Filipino workers, many who were sleeping. Screams of pain and panic could be heard as yet another mortar landed inside the camp.

As we ran into the housing area to provide assistance, well over a hundred of the 1,300 workers were milling in the area, in complete shock, and waiting for yet another impact. Another mortar exploded into an aluminum living container as we yelled for the innocents to seek shelter.

Our immediate effort was to direct survivors to concrete bunkers that would afford relative safety while attempting at the same time to segregate workers who required medical attention. Several men and women stood in complete shock while viewing one of their friends who had been killed instantly with the first explosion. My initial assignment was to remain with the deceased and direct victims and witnesses to a more secure location. When that was accomplished we began the task of evacuating the injured and removing the remains of the deceased.

As military ambulances and assistance arrived, perhaps the most inspirational figure among the carnage was an Army chaplain, a giant of a man, who calmly walked among the Americans and Filipinos, quietly reassuring us all that everything would be OK.

While going about our unpleasant tasks, someone yelled an alert of another "incoming" mortar. We all immediately dived for cover in some area that would provide a degree of protection. During several seconds of an agonizing wait, there was no explosion. We later learned that the "incoming" was in fact an "outgoing" that had been fired by the United States Army against the attacking insurgents, with precision, and with deadly results to the enemy. It was during this attack that I suffered my first and only minor injury in Iraq while diving for cover. While diving to the ground I received numerous small cuts and scratches from landing on the sharp rocks.

The final death toll on May 11th was four Filipino workers killed, several critical injuries, and six who were admitted to the military hospital for shock.

In a response to the incident by President Arroyo of the Philippine government, she stated, "I have instructed the Department of Foreign Affairs and Team Iraq to make a clear-cut assessment of the safety of our civilians employed in U.S. military installations in Iraq. If they cannot be adequately secured, they must be transferred or evacuated to safer areas," she added. Unfortunately, in a war zone there's no "perfect" way to ensure the safety of anyone.

During the following days, the generosity and kindness of the American employees employed by KBR in Iraq would be visible time and again.

Filipino workers would congregate around the three telephones that American personnel had available for maintaining contact with their loved ones. Time after time an American would walk by his or her Filipino counterpart and wordlessly hand a prepaid phone card to ensure the lowly paid victim could contact their loved ones in the Philippines to let them know they had survived.

The attacks on the bus on May 8th and the Filipino compound on the 11th sent one very clear message. The enemy was refining their ability to hit targets with deadly consequences.

On May 12, 2004, we began receiving information on the beheading of an American, Nick Berg. Ironically, our first reports were received from e-mails that were received from the U.S., thanks to the reporting of Fox News.

An e-mail that I sent my wife on May 15, 2004, somewhat provides a clear picture of the life we were experiencing at Camp Anaconda.

> This morning we took our biggest attack yet. We estimate that 12-15 mortars came in. Some didn't explode so now we're having "controlled" blasts every little while when the explosive guys locate and detonate them. There were no major injuries, just a minor one.

The last mortar made a direct hit in the fuel storage lot, but luckily, failed to create the explosion that we'd all feared for so long.

During this period of time, I had the opportunity to review my old calendar and report of activities from my previous tour of duty in Iraq. In June of the previous year, I'd met Daniel Parker, an American expatriate who'd been hired as a fellow security coordinator. I'd met Dan at the Kuwait Airport and had subsequently taken him to the Iraqi border where he'd been placed in the care of a military convoy that was destined for Baghdad. Just the week before, Dan had been killed in Baghdad when his vehicle hit an IED. I remember Parker as a man who was excited about the prospect of serving his country in Baghdad.

Billy Lewis and I seemed to always be together when mortars started falling on Anaconda. Working with him was a comforting aspect in the daily problems we faced. As a team we seemed to handle the stress of incoming mortars and the explosions with humor. We managed to get our work completed, and perhaps of utmost importance, we weren't injured during any of the major attacks.

Lewis continuously surprised me with his logic. On one occasion he jumped in the SUV and informed me that we needed to get to the PX as quickly as possible. The reason? He'd decided that since we spent so much of our time sitting in bunkers, we needed to buy lawn chairs that would make our waiting out the explosions more comfortable.

On one occasion I handed Billy one of the highest compliments that could be paid in a war-infested zone. There was a small lake near our office that contained nothing but sludge, sewage, and solid waste that was collected from the hundreds of sewage containers around Camp Anaconda. I went to the area, tied a handkerchief around my face so I could get closer, and placed a sign that proclaimed the area as "Lake Lewis." When Billy Lewis saw the sign he immediately posted a "No Fishing" warning on his lake.

Ironically, a TCN driver who was emptying his "honey wagon" into Lake Lewis would miss his gears and drive his sewage truck into the lake where the truck, surrounded by raw sewage, would sink to the door windows while a perplexed TCN sadly looked out of the vehicle.

An e-mail that I sent to Donna on May 31, 2004, summed our daily activities up in just a few sentences.

> It's what we in the trade call a scorcher today. It's around 110 degrees and a good day to remain in the air conditioning. Unfortunately, we've had to go up to the convoy transport yard to make our little Turkish guys quit hitting each other. Those "kids" are just incorrigible, but we're slowly but surely getting control of their tempers since they refuse to get control of them on their own.

In June, 2004 my best friend and former partner from the Prince George's County, Maryland, police department arrived at Camp

Anaconda. I'd referred Bob Derfler to Joe Brown, who'd once again worked his never-ending magic and gotten Bob hired as a security technician.

I had previously sent Derfler a list of items to bring.

> Bob:
> Bring a comfortable pair of work boots.
> Bring a laundry bag.
> Bring several pairs of jeans and shirts.
> Bring a new ass, so when they shoot yours off, you'll have a spare.
> Bring 600 copies of *Revenge Served Cold*, by Elmer L. Snow.
> Bring 600 books of *Overkill— A Detective's Story*, by Elmer L. Snow.

Before he departed Kuwait for Anaconda, I sent a somewhat facetious e-mail that was designed to welcome Bob to his new home in Balad.

> Mr. Derfler
> We're pleased to welcome your pending arrival to Camp Anaconda, Iraq, the best kept secret in the Middle East Theater. This e-mail will serve as our notification that you've been accepted to our exclusive resort.
> **"Camp Anaconda"** is truly known as a place you can call home. We're located in a fashionable suburb, approximately two hours north of Baghdad, and within a short three-hour drive of the scenic Euphrates River.
> **"Restaurante DeFAC"** The cuisine at Camp Anaconda is simply referred to as superb. We boast of our two major restaurants that are located within

minutes of the KBR Four Star Hotel and Golf Club. The fare is dietician approved to ensure our guests remain healthy throughout their stay at our resort.

"Medical Facilities" Our in-house medical staff is fully qualified to meet your every need; whether it is an aspirin for an "after night" celebration, or to provide unlimited Viagra for our discriminating guests. We realize that most of our guests are spending the majority of their days on our 18-hole, Arnold Palmer-Designed Golf Course; therefore, we have opened evening hours should you wish to privately consult with a member of our medical staff.

"Security" While at Camp Anaconda, you'll always be aware of the excellent security staff we provide, and who reside on premises as an added precaution in deterring criminal activity. To better serve our patrons, we also provide nightly helicopter patrols to ensure our guests are not disturbed by ground attacks.

"Evening Activities" Camp Anaconda Resort and Golf Club boasts a nightly fireworks display which some guests have stated "it's to die for." We gather nightly on, and in, our cement observation wings to ensure our guests have a firsthand view of this unsurpassed pyrotechnic extravaganza. We promise our guests your heart will leap to your throat during this major event.

"Shopping" Anaconda Resorts has availability of a major AFES Department Store (PX) where you can shop for items that range from designer shirts to light food fare. For our discriminating "non alcoholic" consumers, we do provide non-alcoholic beverages.

"Lake Lewis at Anaconda" is our own fisherman's paradise. The water remains at a constant 87 degrees and fishing is allowed along the sandy shoreline. You may want to swim in this aquatic wonder, or just sit on the shore with a close friend and watch the ripples in the soft luminescent waves. (Note—Boogie Boards may be obtained at our AFES Department Store.

Yes, Bob, paradise and those seven virgins are waiting for your arrival aboard our chartered flight from Kuwait.

Yours truly,

Elmer

On June 17, 2004, I went to the flight section at Camp Anaconda and scheduled my travel for a pending vacation back in Florida. I was scheduled to depart Balad on June 27th, fly to Kuwait, then depart Kuwait on June 30, 2004. Another KBR employee was killed during the day and a meeting of KBR personnel was scheduled for the following morning to announce what had happened to our employee. It was a welcome change not to get the news from Fox.

Billy Lewis and I had supervised the departure of our American convoy drivers during the early morning and just miles from Camp Anaconda our driver had been killed when he hit an Improvised Explosive Device that was hidden in the roadway.

June 19th brought new greetings from the enemy who lurked outside the camp. Before leaving my living container to report to work, we'd experienced five incoming mortars.

Chapter 22

During the first part of September 2004 I was advised that on September 8th I would oversee the security of a rap group, 50 Cent and the G-Unit, who would be coming to Camp Anaconda to perform for the troops. I'd never even heard of 50 Cent and although welcoming the opportunity for a new challenge, I, a 61-year-old father, could have cared less about attending the concert. Let's just say that I was raised with Elvis and would die with Elvis. But, as they say in the business, "the show must go on."

During the afternoon of September 7th, the advance team who would be setting up all of the sound systems for the event arrived at Anaconda. They weren't on the ground for an hour before my security team was hustling them into a bunker because of an incoming mortar that made a lot of noise, yet did no damage.

I did learn from one of my security specialists that Curtis Jackson, known as 50 Cent, would undoubtedly be wearing his trademark bulletproof vest when he arrived. This was consoling inasmuch as the rest of us who would provide the security would be dressed in kind.

In preparing for the concert it was my responsibility to ensure that our guests would not be injured. This was emphasized by a member of the USO who came with the advance team.

On September 8th my detail met a military flight as it arrived at the Balad Air Terminal. Out walked Curtis Jackson, better known to his fans as "50 Cent," his group known as the "G-Unit" and an Italian bodyguard whose hands were so big that they should have had military serial numbers tattooed across the knuckles. Curtis was wearing his vest and actually was a nice guy. I especially appreciated him because he was willing to travel into an extremely high risk area to entertain hundreds of troops who'd arrived early to enjoy the show.

Because of my own background in personal protection I realized the importance of not trying to interfere with the work of 50's own bodyguard. But, I immediately noted that he, the bodyguard, wasn't drinking water and with a temperature of 115 degrees, water was as important as the ability to dodge mortars when "One Shot" got bored. For over two hours I encouraged the escort to consume water, rather than get dehydrated. He continually refused the offer of water.

While 50 Cent and G-Unit entertained the soldiers in the mid-day heat, 50's bodyguard fainted dead away. He would be sick for the remainder of the day.

In all fairness to Curtis Jackson, the G-Unit, and even the bodyguard, who proved to be six foot five in the shoulders and six point five in the head, the American troops loved the concert.

After the group departed I sent Donna an e-mail before calling it a day.

The day is slowing and I can see that sleep and a hopefully comfortable night is in the future. Balad, as has stood for 1,000 years, remains standing. The lovely polluted river continues flowing through the twinkling 25-watt lights of the city. All is good and peace remains in Iraq.

Meanwhile, in Iraq, the natives have fired their bright arrows through the twilight of the setting sun. Injuries mount in some forlorn village where the word Jihad flows at the tips of the native tongues. And, taxi cabs run into the darkness of the night, carrying explosives, yet I am at peace knowing that my lovely wife is in Florida, lying on what used to be my couch.

Chapter 23

Despite the days and nights that represented hours of boredom that were followed by minutes of sheer panic, things seemed to go along their merry way. Billy Lewis and I had gotten into the mode of just enjoying everything we could about life, and our surroundings. Luckily for both of us, whenever we corresponded with our wives through e-mail, or the occasional telephone calls, they seemed to appreciate our humor and life seemed great. We felt real sorrow for those dozens of TCN drivers who would leave the gates of Camp Anaconda, never to be heard from again. We were aware that the short drive from our camp to Baghdad was claiming a lot more lives than anyone will ever know about. On a daily basis we would photograph damage to returning trucks and have the drivers tell us about a truck in front of, or behind them, that had not managed to escape an attack.

The entire security department was shocked in May 2004 when Dan Parker, a security coordinator assigned in Baghdad, was killed by an IED while traveling from the Green Zone, along Purple Heart Highway to the Baghdad International Airport. I remembered picking Dan up at Kuwait International Airport when he first came to work for KBR and had cleared him from the Kuwaiti border when he crossed into Iraq. Kerry Miller, a security manager who worked out of the KBR Government Operations Office in Arlington, Virginia, sent a very moving review of a memorial service that was held for Dan.

The release of information, even in-house, that provided details of KBR employees who were injured or killed while serving their country was almost nonexistent. We, the security coordinators, would initiate reports and forward them up our respective chain of commands. We'd seldom hear a follow-up that was provided by Halliburton or their subsidiary. Several of us wondered if Kerry Miller had gone on his own to keep the employees in the field informed.

Because of all the incoming attacks from mortars and rocket-propelled grenades, many employees, both TCNs and American expatriates began quitting their jobs to return to the safety of the United States. I explained to Donna, in an e-mail, why I was remaining.

> I had a bit of a problem getting to sleep last night. You see, my little living container is on the first row, closest to the enemy fence. The one advantage is there's a massive cement bunker that mortars have to come across, and then immediately drop. In short, my odds are better than many others who're right out in the open. I am concerned about our office building because from outside the fence, the Filipino camp is on a direct line with our office complex. And, none of these buildings are fortified to the extent that they would even slow a mortar down. We're very dependent on the military sentries to stay alert. There have been some instances of where the fences were cut which indicates some sentries aren't always on the job. As a matter of fact, two of the service personnel are in deep trouble for having sex while on guard duty in the towers.

Because some of the security coordinators in my group were becoming depressed, I decided to write a "fictitious" Theater Transportation Movement Security Newsletter for Camp Anaconda.

Easter Plans in Preparation

TTM Security has one again taken the lead role in overseeing preparations for the upcoming 2005 Easter Parade. A new event that is planned for the big day is the IED (Improvised Egg Device) hunt. Our Iraqi brothers have agreed that their devices this Easter will be dyed and we will have an extended hunt that goes from Anaconda to Baghdad. The soldier or expatriate finding the biggest device will be given an LWOP choice of Tikrit, Scania, or Cedar.

The Chairman of the Easter Committee, Shane Irwin states, "This year the entire committee has decided that the Iraqi responsible for painting the winning IED will be given a pig to go with his seven virgins and promise of paradise.

Alcoholics Anonymous Struggles for Membership

The Camp Anaconda Chapter of AA isn't seeing the increase in membership they had anticipated when the chapter was formed. Spokesperson for the group, Billy Lewis, who is known inside the group as "Hi, I'm Billy and I'm an alcoholic," says that he feels the lack of response from problem drinkers is because they're not allowed to carry their coolers to meetings.

PX Stocks New DVDs

The Anaconda PX has obtained a limited number of the first-run movie *Porky Does Balad*.

This movie features Saddam Hussein's voice as Porky.

All moviegoers will remember Saddam in his starring role in *Porky of Arabia*, the gripping story of Porky Pig and his life in an underground bunker in Tikrit.

Items for Sale
Three Motorola radios for sale. Slightly scratched from having owner's initials scratched off. The pre-owned radios will provide hours of intelligence information. Know who and where your friends are at all times. Contact Elmer in room 20.

Obituaries
Ahmed, a Turkish driver who was a frequent guest of TTM Security, passed suddenly; very, very suddenly on May 29, 2004, while en route to his home in Adana, Turkey. Mr. Ahmed ran into the roadway when he observed his missing flatbed truck going north on Main Supply Route, Tampa. Ahmed ran into the path of a Stryker that was escorting a KBR convoy comprised of 87 trucks. Survivors include Mrs. Ahmed and Ahmed's former best friend, Mustapha. Ahmed's new life partner, Shane Irwin, requests that in lieu of flowers, cash donations may be sent to the "Shane Irwin Foundation" at Camp Anaconda, Iraq.

Fashion News
William F. "Billy" Lewis has been observed wearing some very nice threads around the camp. In view of the fact that this is a promotional year, the former electrical guru, turned security coordinator, has wisely invested in several pairs of pants, a sport coat, and a matching raccoon tie. Sources had told this reporter that Christine Lewis, Billy's wife, found an outlet near Rosharon, Texas, that specializes in "hotel pants" that feature a lot of ballroom.

One thing that Lewis and I insisted on. If we were going to be beaten down on occasion, we'd use our somewhat perverse humor to bring us back to the task of dealing with death and destruction.

Meanwhile, Bob Derfler had found his favorite activity in Anaconda. He'd visited every one of the dining facilities and had determined which of the facilities had his favorite foods on any given night. Bob was not going to be cheated out of a meal. In fact, the only time he'd ever catch a bad mood was when a mortar was fired at dinner time.

On Wednesday, June 16, 2004, Sergeant Arthur Mastrapa of the United States Army Reserve's 351st Military Police Company went to the PX at Anaconda. Mastrapa and two other soldiers were enjoying the break in their duties when three 127-millimeter rockets landed at the doorway of the Post Exchange. Sergeant Mastrapa and the other two soldiers were killed by the explosion. Twenty-five other soldiers and civilians were injured in the attack. There were several ironies involved in the death of this Florida M.P. who lost his life.

First, he was from Apopka, Florida, not a long way from where I lived near Tampa. Secondly, he was scheduled to rotate out of the area within one or two days. Lastly, I was returning to Florida on my scheduled vacation. I flew from Camp Anaconda to Baghdad accompanying the flag-covered coffin of the sergeant. I would be in Sun City Center, watching on television, as the remains of Sergeant Mastrapa returned to Florida.

My only comfort that I could relay to his family is the fact that on June 22nd, the United States Army provided their customary care and professionalism as they transported the sergeant to the aircraft and secured his casket as several of us said prayers in his behalf. We waited to board the military aircraft while members of the 351st M.P.s secured the casket of Mastrapa aboard the plane.

It was a real break to return home for a few days.

Chapter 24

On June 22, 2004, I took a military flight from Camp Anaconda, landed briefly in Baghdad, and then flew to Kuwait where I would process through the human resources department for my return flight for vacation in Florida. The passengers on the flight bowed their heads in respect upon viewing the flag-draped coffin.

I would only be at home for a couple of days before we drove to the Florida Keys, accompanied by our parrots, Bogart and Daisy, who were accompanied by "their" pet parakeet, Zippy.

It's amazing how Florida soothes the soul. I did note that I had problems sleeping, perhaps because I was subconsciously waiting for a mortar to land.

At the time, Joe Brown was having his own rest and recuperation period near Crystal River in Florida. Although we talked by phone, we were unable to meet for the bottle of Jack Daniel's we'd previously planned on sharing.

While on vacation, Billy Lewis would provide me with regular updates that normally advised that the mortars were still flying and the expatriates were still ducking.

A vacation, under any other name, is still an excellent opportunity to review situations and begin to find solutions to problems that may exist.

As I thought about my experiences in the Middle East I began to truly realize that terrorism is a "device" or "tactic" that won't go away in my lifetime, and probably many future lifetimes of my descendants. As had been pointed out in one of the many schools on terrorism that I'd previously attended, "Terrorism is theater, and the world is the stage."

I began to realize that the days in which I'd personally witnessed the youth of Iraq trying to slow convoys to obtain food, water, candy and the like had taught the insurgents and terrorists new ways to create an opportunity to attack. Iraq serves as a training opportunity for terrorists to either refine, or develop new methods to be used in the future to further the cause and goals of hatred.

When I'd first entered the world of corporate security, the threat to executives was the potential of a ransom kidnapping. Iraq was perfecting the technique. They were also perfecting the "art" of random murder. After all, I could remember the early 1980s when a motorcycle in South America would pull adjacent to a vehicle and a passenger on the motorcycle would open fire, injuring or killing the target. In Iraq, where there were fewer motorcycles, a taxi would often be used to emulate the scenario with the same deadly results.

The dangers of homicide by suicide bombings had increased drastically during my time in Iraq. The fact that there are so many so-called "martyrs" who are willing to sacrifice their life to kill a handful of others had started in Baghdad and was spreading throughout the country like an Oklahoma wildfire.

Perhaps the only disappointing aspect of my vacation was the receipt of an e-mail from Billy Lewis that Shane Irwin had quit his job as a security manager with KBR and had returned to North Carolina.

Shane had been one of the best supervisors I'd worked for while in my role as a security coordinator for KBR. The security role at Camp Anaconda had been divided into two groups with separate functions. Shane, Derfler, Lewis and I were assigned to the Theater Transportation Movement, an assignment which dealt primarily with issues facing the drivers as they moved supplies throughout Iraq. A separate KBR security detail was assigned to "Force Protection" issues of camp life. We'd known for some time that the supervisors handling force protection were attempting to have all the units incorporated as one "team." I personally felt the concept was a good one as it would ensure all of KBR security were working off of one page. However, the force protection group was being used for assignments that they hadn't been hired for. In short, they were doing many of the tasks that were solely delegated to our military personnel.

Shane had complained on many occasions that following mortar attacks, KBR security was being used to investigate the origin of the attacks to report to the military. In short, during actual attacks, our unarmed and unprotected personnel were being exposed to dangers they hadn't been hired, or trained for. Irwin had become extremely vocal about the issue and all of the people who reported to him knew that he was making every effort to ensure we weren't unnecessarily placed in "harm's way."

As the political infighting became more vocal, Shane realized that he was not going to gain the support to have security conduct only the role they had been hired for. Rather than see any of his personnel injured by bad management, he chose to leave the company.

The force protection side of security was also managed by a great team. Although I agreed with Shane's reasoning, I still felt that security should be under a team concept, rather than an "I" concept. But, I did not relish the thought of returning to Camp Anaconda and doing a job that the American military was responsible to do. One thing that those of us recognized on the TTM side of security was that we had lost a great manager who had given up his job because of his own integrity and principles.

When I departed Florida to return to Iraq, I learned that the new procedure would be to fly into Dubai, be processed, and then catch a military flight to Camp Anaconda. With just minor problems and issues that are normally associated with flying, this was accomplished with a minor detour into Baghdad where it would be necessary to be cleared through customs. The Iraqis had assumed the customs duty at Baghdad International Airport and it was apparent by their inspections that the new policy was giving the Iraqis the opportunity to begin flexing their muscles. All in all, it wasn't a bad experience with the exception that customs officials thought I was bringing too many cigarettes into their country. Thanks to American personnel who were working with the Iraqis, the problem was quickly resolved and I returned to the plane for my continuation flight to Balad.

Chapter 25

Upon return to Camp Anaconda I learned of another new procedure that had taken place since my return for vacation. In the past, security personnel were met at their airplane by coworkers who would quickly expedite them back to their assigned billets. A change that had taken place meant all passengers had to ride a bus to a KBR staging area, be processed, then worry about carrying their luggage, usually comprised of a couple of trunks and a suitcase, back to their quarters. It was just another indication of the changes that continued to take place in our assignment.

True to form, a mortar was fired outside the fence and landed near the airfield area as a proper welcome to all the personnel, both those returning from vacation, and new hires that were reporting for their initial assignment. Kuwait was no longer a point of entering into Iraq. Personnel flew directly from Dubai to their assignment, via Baghdad International Airport (BIAP).

Chapter 26

My return to Camp Anaconda brought new areas of responsibility for me. I was designated to provide security briefings for new hires who'd just been assigned to the camp. I would learn that this would involve a minimum of three briefings weekly to ensure new personnel were briefed before beginning their assignments.

There were times when the security briefing alone was enough to convince a new employee to return to the comfort of their homes in the United States.

Billy Lewis was still working faithfully and he'd received assurance that within a few days he'd be promoted from a security technician position to that of a security coordinator. There was no one in the base who was more deserving of a promotion than Lewis.

Meanwhile, my friend Bob Derfler had decided that four months of Iraq was enough for him. When I returned, "Derf" advised me that he would be going through the demobilization procedures within two weeks.

An e-mail back to my wife described the activities I'd returned to.

> Good Morning
> The official Camp Anaconda temperature at 4:00 PM, (Balad Time) is 118 degrees. Need I say more?
> Our neighbor camp at Talil was hit today and hit hard. I guess two VBIED (Vehicle Borne Improvised Exploding Devices) were used. I guess we could simplify the whole thing by saying they were car bombs. I understand that several Iraqis bought the farm, but we received nothing on our personnel or the military being injured.
> It's been a pretty quiet day here. I guess we received four or five incoming mortars last night, but no reports of injury or damage. I heard the first one, sat in the bunker with Billy for a while, then returned to bed when the "all clear" sounded. As tradition goes, I slept through the remainder of the incoming bombs.

Since I knew that Bob Derfler was going to be leaving the area in a short time, I took the opportunity to have some fun by sending a somewhat facetious e-mail to our counterparts who we maintained particularly close contact with.

> Guys
> I just wanted to give you some insight on our "Security Boy," Bob Derfler.
> First, the F. in his name stands for Frago. It's Robert Frago Derfler.
> When Bob says that he's served in Viet Nam, he means that he made the popcorn and got the beer during the movie, *Good Morning, Viet Nam.*

Bob's favorite dramatic actors are Curly, Moe, and Larry.

For years, Bob thought that "lock and load" meant locking his front door and going out drinking.

As a baby, Bob loved putting his foot in his mouth. He's continued this practice for over 50 years.

Bob is the only man in Maryland whose been charged with spousal abuse for mistreating his inflatable doll.

As a cop, Bob was shot six times. Every wound was determined to be self-inflicted. All six shots hit his foot, but it was later determined he'd been aiming for his head.

As a police negotiator, Bob walked into a bank that was being robbed by a suspect who was armed with a sawed-off shotgun. Bob's first negotiating words were "we need to talk, give me a shot." The ambulance arrived in record time.

Needless to say, Derfler would continue with his lifelong ability to get even with me. Perhaps that's why we'd managed to remain friends for close to 30 years.

Chapter 27

Being back at Camp Anaconda wasn't bad in the beginning, but as time progressed I began to really feel a need to be back in the U.S. with family and friends. After Bob Derfler left I started to realize that I'd spent enough time in an environment where the insurgents were becoming more and more proficient in pursuing their deadly games.

The incoming mortars were increasing on a daily basis, and the convoys we sent along the roads of Iraq were being attacked with a new vengeance. It wasn't at all unusual to hear and feel the vibration of an incoming mortar, retreat to a cement bunker, then wait endlessly for a siren to announce an all clear.

When I attempted to check on the status of my security clearance, I learned that someone in the corporate offices had decided not to submit the paperwork. This would ensure that I would not have my security clearance by the end of my contract, and would undoubtedly not be able to remain in country for an extended tour of duty. Meanwhile, the mortars kept on landing with deadly consequences.

On September 15, 2004, I decided to hang up my Kevlar helmet and vest and return home. At that time I decided to write an article entitled "A View from Iraq," that would express my feelings on that day in my life. That article is now a book.

It is September 15th and after spending an accumulative total of over a year in Iraq, it's time to return to the relative security of Sun City Center, Florida.

There are two words that immediately come to mind when I look back on my experience in the reconstructive phase of Operation Iraqi Freedom. They are: honor and privilege. It has been an honor to observe our American Forces in the performance of their duties and it is a privilege to write about them. I will not neglect the army of civilians who also risk their own lives daily to support our military forces.

Immediately after arriving in Kuwait, I was called upon in my security role to meet a helicopter that was making an emergency transport of an American civilian driver to a tented medical facility. It soon became apparent to me that there was only one constructive thing I could do. In view of the condition of the victim, I elected to just sit next to him in the intensive care facility. I imagined that my only alternative would be, at some point, to inform the next of kin that someone who cared was with their loved one when he expired, and that he was not in pain. Miraculously, and with the expertise of military medical personnel, that driver is somewhere in the U.S. and hopefully enjoying life as I intend to do.

Even a vacation from a war zone can become a bittersweet experience.

On June 16, 2004, Sergeant Arthur S. Mastrapa, a military policeman from Apopka, Florida, was tragically killed in a mortar attack at my base in Balad, Iraq. It was my privilege and honor to share a portion of Arthur's last flight out of Iraq.

A proud new mother could not have held her baby with more care than the manner in which an Honor Guard from the United States Army handled the flag-covered casket of Mastrapa. And, this was not just Balad, but also in Kuwait when another Honor Guard Unit was waiting at three in the morning to delicately remove his casket for return to his loved ones.

Yesterday, September 14th, I was again summoned to the hospital in Balad. Another American civilian, an employee of Black Water Security, had driven over a land mind, just minutes from the safer environment of our camp. He did not survive.

There are so many stories, perhaps a book that I will write when I return to Florida next week. Whatever I write, it will be my privilege to honor the memory of those who serve in Iraq. I have had an excellent view of Iraq. I was there!

Chapter 28

Since my return from Iraq, I've traded "God's Waiting Room" in Florida for "God's *Living* Room" in the Smoky Mountains of Tennessee. I've given up the life of a security specialist for the life of an ERA Realtor. What I haven't given up, and something that increases on a daily basis, is my frustration with political figures who want the United States Government to get out of Iraq before the job is finished. In my opinion, too many Americans and members of the Coalition Forces have died for us to stop our fight against terrorism on the very lands where terrorism was born and raised.

Perhaps there is something rewarding that comes with age. That's the ability to remember incidents from the past, such as kidnapping of Americans in Beirut, Lebanon, or Iran, killing of an American soldier during a plane hijacking, the bombing of the U.S.S. *Cole*, bombing attacks on American Embassies, and more recently, the events of September 11, 2001. And, in far too many cases, no retaliatory efforts were ever made, regardless of the political party in power.

I had the opportunity during my tenure in Iraq to meet many Kurds who had individually lost dozens of members of their respective families to the weapons of mass destruction used by a mad dictator. Yet, certain members of our own United States Congress delight in stating that no weapons of mass destruction were ever located. Perhaps it's because they were used against the Kurds or Iranians? I personally observed many individuals known commonly as "Third Country Nationals" who lost their lives to terrorists along the roads of Iraq, not to mention the hundreds of American soldiers, coalition soldiers, and American expatriates who were victims of terrorism.

As I write this book I realize the current trend is to demand that our remaining soldiers in Iraq be brought home, or that a time table be initiated for their return.

Our troops are similar to farmers who have planted the seeds of democracy in a country that has never had the opportunity to savor the wonderful taste of a delicacy called democracy. But, it's a crop that when planted, it has to be nurtured, cared for, carefully cultivated, and given the chance to grow. Would bringing our "farmers" home too soon allow others to destroy that fine crop that so many hands have sown, through blood, sweat, tears, injury and death? And, what would happen to those Iraqis who've joined us in bringing a "new" crop onto an old field? Too many sacrifices, it appears to me, have been made by our forces to just throw down the tools and walk out of the farm. Too many lives have been sacrificed for us to declare victory, and walk away while the crop can't be cultivated by those we planted the crop for. My opinion of a time table for leaving Iraq is to do so when the crop is fertile.

Perhaps if some of our illustrious politicians spent a few weeks or months in Iraq, rather than a quick trip for a photo opportunity, then they would better understand that the right time to get our of Iraq cannot come until "it's the right time." Leave time constraints up to football games, not wars.

In November, 2003 I met Yasin T. al-Jibouri when he returned to Zakho, Iraq, after spending many years in exile in the United States. Yasin had returned to participate in the reconstruction of his country that had been devastated by the hand of tyranny and ravages of war. He had originally left Baghdad under the umbrella of darkness to escape being yet another victim of Saddam Hussein.

After my own return to Florida I accepted employment as a reporter for the *Observer News* in Ruskin, Florida. I subsequently called on Yasin, via e-mail, to provide an eyewitness account of the elections in Iraq.

His article will hopefully enlighten my readers regarding the importance of the two elections and installation of a new government in Iraq. In my own mind, I believe the comments made by Mr. al-Jibouri reflect that he, along with all Americans, want our soldiers out of Iraq, but realizes that we're still needed by those whose country we're helping to rebuild.

Election Thoughts
By: Yasin T. al-Jibouri
Finally the Iraqi general elections are over. Thank God! Too much has been said about them, about postponing or even canceling them altogether, but no more talk anymore. And, YES, I had the opportunity to participate in them. Up to the last day I thought I could not, because my official documents proving my Iraqi citizenship were simply not issued to me yet, with the exception of a lone document that proved to be an "election saver!" The whole process took a few seconds. No fuss, no lining up in a long row as I'd expected, and no terrorist attacks. Everything was smooth sailing.

Speaking of terrorist attacks, I must admit I was very much concerned about the fact that my house is located across the street from the polling center where I cast my vote. I told myself that since my wife and our unborn daughter are far away, I would not mind being the scapegoat, should anything happen, God forbid. That was a fatal thought, but this is exactly how I felt. Two or three National Guardsmen kept their eyes on the school and made sure no vehicles passed nearby. Roadblocks were placed around the polling center, the small elementary school facing my house, but beyond that, children formed soccer teams here and there and enjoyed playing in the empty streets.

Yes, I must admit, I felt relieved to see the elections being held and coming to a successful conclusion. I was amazed at seeing so many women participating in the elections. Some of them, to my surprise, did not know how to read and write, yet they were determined to enjoy their right to vote, something which they had never done before. And I saw elderly men and women, too, walking with canes, their backs bent, barely making their way on the uneven cracked pavement of streets that have never been coated or repaired, so that it is riddled with potholes. I put my hand on my heart as I watched an old man with a bent back moving his cane from one pothole to another, fearing he might slip and fall. But he too proved to be tough. You see, resolution grants people strength from an unknown source. I have always known my people, the Iraqi people, to be quite strong and resilient; otherwise, how can you explain their survival during all their ordeals, trials and tribulations, wars of attrition, even when more than 40 nations ganged up against them in 1991 in order to break them up, to get them out of Kuwait, even after so many bombs rained on their once beautiful capitol, Baghdad, spreading death and destruction everywhere.

Why did all those men and women take the risk to go to the polling centers? Speaking for myself, and I think my reason for going there may not be different from that of many others. I can say I went there prompted by my convictions that voting is a right that must never be relinquished, a weapon that must be wisely used, a tool to bring the right person to the right position. I voted when I was in the United States, my second home, where I learned the importance of voting, and now, I am voting in my country of birth. It is a good feeling. As for others to whom I spoke, inquiring about the reasons why they voted, these folks told me they were prompted by many common incentives; the desire to see some real positive change in Iraq, to see an end to an unprecedented administrative corruption, to theft of public funds on a scale never before seen, to an end to bribery, favoritism, partisanship, to bring about public officials who will be concerned about their image and reputations, officials who will not seek excuses for current national crises, shortages of potable water, only a few hours of electrical power a day, huge increases in fuel prices and in the prices of almost all other commodities, almost a total absence of the most basic public services such as street cleaning and lighting, garbage collection, telephone connections, a civilized traffic system...and, above all, the absence of security and stability. The latter has been on the minds of most people in Iraq (with the exception of perhaps people living in Kurdistan Province who enjoy plenty of electrical power) since the U.S. Forces set foot in Iraq, since they were welcomed, and since the welcome turned into a bitter disappointment when the "allied" or "coalition" forces paid no heed to the security needs in Iraq, Leaving Iraqi borders open to the intruders and terrorists, shifting the security responsibility to a skeleton Iraqi police force that could not protect itself, much less protect its citizens. Many voters told me they wanted to see Iraqi army and police as well as security forces doing their job to protect Iraq and the Iraqis at home and everywhere else, securing the borders, eliminating the terrorists, both domestic and imported, and letting the Iraqi individual feel his/her dignity and prestige. The said they had seen enough humiliation, and it is time they breathed the fresh air of freedom. Some said they wanted to see Iraqis building Iraq, since no one cares about Iraq other than the Iraqis. Grand Ayatollah Ali al-Sistani placed so much emphasis on voting that in one of his statements he indicated the following: "If one does not go to vote, he/she will have to account for it before God on the Day of Judgment," a very strong statement, indeed.

Now the elections are over, attention goes to who will hold the reins of government in his hands. To many to whom I spoke, this does not matter much. Most of them said to me, "It really does not matter who comes to rule so long as he is accepted by the majority of the people for his fairness, justice, and equity, and not to use this post to rob the public coffers."

Plenty of such robbing has been going on here in Iraq recently and during Saddam's regime and this has to stop. Perhaps the election results will stop it. Iraqis very much hope so, and I do too.

Let us keep our fingers crossed!!

Yasin T. al-Jibouri

Chapter 29
Conclusion

There have been many lessons learned from Iraq that will have an effect on military and civilian operations in a war zone for the indeterminate future of man. And, terrorism has already been successfully used in the United States, as well as throughout the world, so we should always be prepared with the knowledge that it will most assuredly happen again.

If one soldier, one expatriate, or one citizen benefits from the following observations, then my book was well worth the investment of time and remembrance of horrors of living in a war zone.

During my time in Iraq, a military convoy departed the area of the Turkish border in northern Iraq. The purpose was to escort several hundred fuel trucks that made a daily trip from the border to the area of Mosul, Iraq, where the supplies would be offloaded for coalition forces. At approximately 7:30 AM an orange and white painted taxi passed the lead vehicle, an LMTV truck. All seemed well until the trunk of the taxi suddenly opened and an Iraqi male began firing at the truck with an AK-47 rifle. One soldier was shot in the foot prior to the assailant's negotiating a sudden U-turn and making good their escape. It should not go unnoticed that during this period of time, American media was extensively covering the aftermath and trial of two snipers in the D.C. area who had randomly killed innocents while concealed in the trunk of their vehicle. Was this a coincidence? Perhaps it was. But the fact remains that terrorists have always copied acts that were successful. And, crusaders, crazies, and criminals in Iraq are perfecting the "art of attack" and their successes will undoubtedly be imitated throughout the world in the future.

Iraq presents myriad challenges for the security professionals, many who are currently in Iraq, and for those who will follow during the reconstruction phase, and under the new government in Iraq. Preparedness is definitely a key to survival in this hostile environment. Hopefully, each of us who serves in Iraq can pass on information that will better ensure the safety and security of our counterparts who will serve there in the future.

Despite individual training at defensive driving and counterterrorism driving course there are many areas that training and education doesn't prepare us for. Traveling in a convoy primarily subjects you to the rules of the convoy commander. You will normally place the ability to perform a J-turn or Bootlegger turn on a back burner. The ability to ram a vehicle to remove it from your path, or divert the accuracy of gunfire is paramount for survival. And, as previously mentioned, allowing a vehicle to get between you and the next convoy vehicle in line could be a deadly mistake that you'll not make again. You should also forget the option of driving off of the roadway as an evasive counter measure. Improvised Exploding Devices (IEDs) and land mines that can be covertly placed in minutes preclude the side of the road as a logical escape route.

Beware of what's in the roadway and not in the roadway.

Yes, there's a degree of contradiction there, but it's true. Insurgents have perfected the art of hiding explosives in the roadway.

A pothole might be concealing a land mine just as discarded Coca-Cola cans, plastic bags, dead animals, and plastic water bottles that are never out of view while driving. And, the broken-down vehicle at the side of the road might just contain the explosives that will end your career. In Iraq, and in countries where we learn from Iraq, drive offensively and think defensively.

Overpasses present their own unique challenges. A common practice is to conceal oneself on an overpass, then drop materials onto the roofs or in the paths of oncoming vehicles. One tactic that has been successfully used is suspending a cinder block from a rope during the night time. By adjusting the block to windshield levels, one can be assured of creating damage or injury. One defensive countermeasure is to change lanes quickly when approaching a crossover or while under the overpass.

Another important item to remember is a need to maintain a better ratio of military escorts to the number of vehicles in a given convoy. In northern Iraq it's not unusual for four or five military vehicles to be assigned to escort up to 400 trucks, many carrying highly volatile fuel while others are carrying necessities for coalition forces. This practice almost ensures that there could easily be 20 miles distance between crew served weapons. It's not unusual for a tractor trailer to be hijacked out of a protected convoy, and no one becomes aware of the incident until the convoy reaches its destination. In southern Iraq convoys travel with a more realistic ratio of 25-30 convoy vehicles with 2-3 military escorts. Although there are fewer attacks even these smaller convoys are not without their own problems.

Situational awareness in a convoy could mean your life. This is especially true when one is behind or in front of fuel or natural gas trucks. These are soft targets which could easily stop an entire convoy if struck by the enemy. Try to be assigned to a location that is closest to an armed military escort.

For any security professional who might be involved in transportation movements which depend on military escorts, there is a major issue to be mindful of. If you're in a country that utilizes drivers from "Third World countries," be mindful that these drivers don't view their vehicles as a potential weapon. Their truck is their sole support and to lose the truck through an accident or attack can establish a lifelong economic disaster. In short, the vehicle that may be in front or behind you in a convoy is much more likely to stop during an attack rather than make an attempt to distance them from the prevailing danger. Any professionally trained security driver knows that the vehicle they are operating is only an extension of the security arsenal they possess. It too, is your weapon.

Those of us who have specialized in the field of executive protection are trained from our first day of employment or training that a good security advance is not only necessary, it's completely indispensable. Iraq has proven that there are situations and environments where conducting an advance is not feasible. This leaves the security operative with conducting his or her advance as they travel along. You should constantly evaluate the surroundings, look for potential attack sites, and make the determination of what you will do if something occurs. Keep abreast of current intelligence for the area where you're required to travel. At one time, in Iraq, there wasn't a problem related to kidnapping. If someone attacked you, your team, or convoy, there wasn't intent to take a prisoner or hostage. Their only goal was to destroy, kill, and escape. This theory changed and kidnapping became a valuable tool in the hands of terrorists. In some cases, escape isn't one of the considerations as the prevalent threat of a homicide bomber is always at the forefront of our planning. There again, current intelligence might provide the alert you need to plan your own recourse of action. Good intelligence begins with the first incident and the theory that if it was successful once, it will be tried again.

If traveling with a military convoy you should determine certain information before you begin your journey. Ascertain what the military option will be in the event of an attack! Options may differ with leadership. Some protocols may be to launch an immediate counterattack while others choose to evacuate from the area. If you know what plan of response is in effect, then you won't be surprised if the convoy suddenly stops and engages the attackers, or if they increase speed to expedite from the area. Having this specific information is necessary for you to develop your own survival strategy while on the move.

There isn't enough emphasis that can be placed on the fact that terrorist and guerilla warfare in Iraq continues to be an educational opportunity for others to follow in other parts of the world. We have seen the old "Red Brigade" tactic of two killers on a motorcycle approaching from the left rear and conducting a successful "hit" on the streets of Iraq. It worked in Italy, now it works in Iraq. However, the lack of motorcycles increased the use of small trucks and taxi cabs for this purpose. We, in the security field must be cognizant that someday the deployment of Improvised Exploding Devices will be used in any part of the world, and security practitioners will then recall that the strategy was perfected in Iraq.

Iraq is more than a horrible event we're living through. It's a horrible event that will be repeated, and one that we can learn from that will keep future generations safer.

As Yasin T. al-Jibouri stated, "Let's keep our fingers crossed."

Elmer Snow and Bob Derfler in Balad, Iraq.

Author—Elmer L. Snow in Kuwait

IED Attack on Fuel Transporter in Iraq

Evacuation to Chopper of Syrian truck driver who was saved by
U.S. Army personnel.

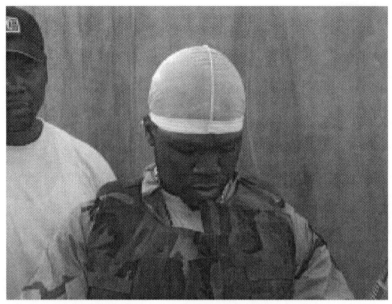

Jackson (50 Cent) at Camp Anaconda, Iraq

50 Cent in Concert at Camp Anaconda, Iraq

American Supply Truck after IED Attack

Entertainers on USO visit to Camp Anaconda

KBR Security Office in Balad, Iraq

PX at Camp Anaconda where Americans Died During Mortar Attack

Kuwait Border Police with Ransom Payoff in Background

Kurdish Funeral Procession in Zakho, Iraq

Small PX at Camp Anaconda, Iraq

Restaurant in Northern Iraq (Kurdistan)

Billy Lewis at Camp Anaconda, Iraq

Printed in the United States
72424LV00002B/304-348